ARISE JERUSALEM!

A FAMILY ADVENT HANDBOOK

YO-CZN-477

PAULIST PRESS

New York, N.Y./Ramsey, N.J./Toronto

ACKNOWLEDGEMENTS

The editor wishes to express gratitude to the designated
publishers for their kind permission to quote from the
following works:

THE CHRISTMAS COOK BOOK by Kathleen Epperson, ©1969,
Nitty Gritty Productions, Concord, California. Used by
permission.

Rousing Song of Praise with gestures: "Sing to the Lord" by
Donald Fishel, © 1974 The Word of God. (Music available from:
Hymn of the Universe or *Songs of Praise, Vol. I,* Servant Music
Distribution Center, 237 North Michigan, Sound Bend, IN
46601.)

Excerpts from the Jerusalem Bible, Copyright ©1966 by Darton,
Longman and Todd, Ltd., and Doubleday and Company, Inc.
Reprinted by permission of the publisher.

Recipe adapted from CHRISTMAS DECORATIONS FOR YOU
TO MAKE by Susan Purdy. Copyright ©1965 by Susan Purdy.
Reprinted by permission of J.B. Lippincott Company.

Library of Congress
Catalog Card Number: 78-70425

ISBN: 0-8091-9179-2

General Editor:
Jean Marie Hiesberger

Art and Design: Emil Antonucci

Published by Paulist Press
Editorial Office: 1865 Broadway, New York, N.Y. 10023
Business Office: 545 Island Road, Ramsey, N.J. 07446

Printed and bound in the
United States of America

CONTENTS

**JOYFUL MYSTERIES
OF THE ROSARY**

HOW TO USE THIS SECTION

These reflections on the Joyful Mysteries lend themselves to a variety of uses both individually and communally. They can be used in whole or in part as a reflection after Communion. If read aloud to a congregation, these reflections can be done effectively by two readers, one reading the text and the other reading the Scripture quotes included here. Readers should practice beforehand to establish proper rhythm and expression.

In small groups, these reflections could serve as the basis for a guided meditation. They could be read accompanied by slides or other visuals. Families who have decided to pray the rosary during Advent could use these reflections during their family prayer time.

Finally, individuals could use these reflections privately, either in conjunction with praying the rosary or as a starting point for personal meditation.

JOYFUL MYSTERIES OF THE ROSARY

J. Janda

INTRODUCTION

in Christ
we see the revelation of God's
tender loving kindness
his absolute unbreakable fidelity
to man

Christ said
no one can come to me
unless the Father draw him

our union
with him in prayer
is the acceptance
of the Father's drawing

it is a revulsion of human values

it is a revulsion of securities

it is a waiting for the Father's touch

it is allowing the Spirit
to become enfleshed in us
with the enigma of who we are

it is an acceptance
of God's love
to be communicated to others

it is a response to Christ's call
to be ministers of reconciliation
between God and man

artists throughout history
have portrayed Mary
holding the Christ
showing him to us
offering him to us

it is hoped that
through these meditations
we may accept
the God-Man
Mary bore for us

THE ANNUNCIATION

*In the sixth month the angel Gabriel was sent by
God to a town in Galilee called Nazareth, to a
virgin betrothed to a man named Joseph, of the
House of David; and the virgin's name was Mary.
He went in and said to her, "Rejoice, so highly
favored! The Lord is with you," She was deeply
disturbed by these words and asked herself what
this greeting could mean, but the angel said to
her, "Mary, do not be afraid; you have won God's
favor. Listen! You are to conceive and bear a son,
and you must name him Jesus. He will be called
Son of the Most High. The Lord God will give him
the throne of his ancestor David; he will rule over
the House of Jacob for ever and his reign will have
no end." Mary said to the angel, "But how can this
come about, since I am a virgin?"*
Luke 1:26-34

how can this be

the Lord calls
he invites

how can this be

the Lord calls
this confuses
this disturbs
how can this be

Mary's first response
was a question

and through the centuries
the reaction is the same

Moses said to God,
"Who am I to go to Pharaoh
and bring the sons of Israel
out of Egypt?" Exodus 3:11

Jeremiah said to God,
"Ah, Lord Yahweh;
look, I do not know how to speak:
I am a child!" Jeremiah 1:6

Isaiah said,
"What a wretched state I am in!
I am lost,
for I am a man of unclean lips
and I live among a people
of unclean lips
and my eyes have seen the King,
Yahweh Sabaoth." Isaiah 6:5

and the reactions
the attitudes
to Christ's call
are the same

how can this be

Lord, depart from me, for I am a sinful man

but Lord, I have had five husbands
and he with whom I live
is not my husband

but Lord, I am a tax-collector

Lord, I am a fisherman

and isn't our reaction the same

Lord, if you really knew
you wouldn't call me

how can you love me
how can you call me

and this is the mystery

*It is not the healthy
who need the doctor
but the sick.*

*Go and learn the meaning of the words:
What I want is mercy, not sacrifice.
And indeed I did not come to call the virtuous,
but sinners.* Matthew 9:12-13

*I tell you,
there will be more rejoicing in heaven
over one repentant sinner
than over ninety-nine virtuous men
who have no need of repentance.* Luke 15:7

Christ has called, we respond

in spite of our past
and fears of the future

can we say with Mary

*I am the handmaid
of the Lord . . .*

*let what you have said
be done to me.* Luke 1:38

can we see our goodness
and accept our goodness

we have come from God's hand
we have been made in his image

can we with Mary
make a prayer of praise

can we remember all
the good things
God has done for us

can we say

*My soul proclaims the greatness of the Lord
and my spirit exults in God my savior . . .
for the Almighty has done great things for me.
Holy is his name . . .* Luke 1:46, 49

THE VISITATION
*Mary set out at that time and went as quickly as
she could to a town in the hill country of Judah.
She went into Zechariah's house and greeted
Elizabeth. Luke 1:39-40*

Mary did not understand
she believed

in faith—she visited
Elizabeth
who was about to give birth

she showed her faith
doing deeds

and Christ's words
tell us the importance
of deeds

I was hungry and you gave me food;
I was thirsty and you gave me drink;
I was a stranger and you made me welcome;
naked and you clothed me,
sick and you visited me,
in prison and you came to see me.
I tell you solemnly,
in so far as you did this to one
of the least of these brothers of mine,
you did it to me. Matthew 25:35-40

If anyone gives so much as a cup of cold water
to one of these little ones . . .
he will most certainly not lose his reward.
Matthew 10:42

a visit
a compliment
a letter
a phone call
a promise kept

little things

Christ told us
would not go
unrewarded

little things
make the quality
of our day

they grace the day
like candle light or
flowers on the table

it is tempting
to get lost in issues
and speculation
but as Therese of Lisieux
reminds us

without deeds
even the sublimest
visions fail

THE NATIVITY

The Word was made flesh,
he lived among us,
and we saw his glory,
the glory that is his
as the only Son of the Father,
full of grace and truth. John 1:14

we are called
to share in God's life

in and through
Jesus Christ

and as the Father
with the Spirit
were known through
Christ's flesh

can we believe that
our bodies can become
instruments
of God's revelation
to others

just as melody
is communicated through
an instrument

we can become
living instruments
of God's mercy
healing, forgiveness

that is what
incarnation means
God being born
in flesh

deep in our traditions
is the story
of Lucifer's fall

Lucifer, pure spirit,

was disgusted with the knowledge
that God would become flesh
that God would become man

and over the centuries
we find repeated
this disgust of the flesh

spirit/matter
soul/body

many would place
a higher value
on spirit
on soul

and they seem to suggest
that we come from God
and go to God
only in spirit

as if we could leave the body
to do this
as a man steps out of his car

the Manichees
the Catharists
the Albigensians
mirror
these attitudes
and
were condemned
as
heretics

can we believe
the truth of Genesis

God saw all he had made,
and indeed it was very good.
Genesis 1:31

and the truth of Wisdom

Yes,
you love all that exists,
you hold nothing of what you have made
in abhorrence,
for had you hated anything,
you would not have formed it.
And how,
had you not willed it,
could a thing persist,
how be conserved
if not called forth by you?
Wisdom 11:24-27

Can we believe
the truth of John

Through him all things came to be,
not one thing had its being but through him.
All that came to be had life in him. John 1:2-3

we must believe in the goodness
of our flesh

God depends on our birth
our life and death
to show his courtesy

his respect to others
as Christ did

he has no healing hands
but ours
no smiles, but ours
no forgiving
words, but ours

can God's Word
become flesh
in us

He came to his own domain
and his own people did not accept him.
But to all who did accept him
he gave power to become children of God,
to all who believe in the name of him
who was born not out of human stock
or urge of the flesh
or will of man
but of God himself. John 1:11-13

can we say with Julian of Norwich

God
of thy goodness
give me thyself
for thou art enough to me
and I may nothing ask
that is less
that may be
full worship to thee
and if I ask anything

that is less
ever me wanteth
but only in thee
have I all

(REVELATIONS OF DIVINE LOVE, ed. Dom Roger
   Hudleston. Burns, Oates and Washbourne;
   London, 1927)

THE PRESENTATION

And when the day came for them to be purified as
laid down by the Law of Moses, they took him up
to Jerusalem to present him to the Lord . . . Luke
2:23

to present to the Lord
means to bless

to bless means
to honor as holy
to give back to God
what he gave to us

we may bless
our friends
our selves
our talents
our children
all that we are
and have

can we bring
all that we sense

all that we know
all of our relationships
to Christ

can we
with Christ
and through Christ
reconcile
all to the Father

He is the image of the unseen God
and the first-born of all creation,
for in him were created
all things in heaven and on earth . . .

. . . God wanted all things to be reconciled
through him and for him,
everything in heaven and everything on earth . . .
Colossians 1:15-20

can we bless the day
and bless the night

can we in Christ
reconcile
all to the Father

let us bless our life
our talents
our friends
let us give them
back to the Father
who gave them to us

let us say the prayer
of Ignatius

Take, O Lord, and receive
all my liberty,
my memory, my understanding,
my entire will.
Whatever I have or hold,
Thou hast given me;
I restore it all to Thee
and surrender it wholly
to be governed by Thy will.
Give me only Thy love
and Thy grace,
and I am rich enough
and ask for nothing more.

adapted from "Suscipe" a traditional prayer

THE FINDING IN THE TEMPLE

Three days later, they found him in the Temple . . .
They were overcome when they saw him, and his
mother said to him, "My child, why have you done
this to us? See how worried your father and I have
been, looking for you."

He then went down with them and came to
Nazareth and lived under their authority. His
mother stored up all these things in her heart.
Luke 2:46-52 (shortened)

how can this be
joy in suffering
again—mystery

and our sufferings
the disappointments
the discouragements
the jealousies
the hates
the hurts
our fears
our confusions
all those things
which diminish
which wear us

can we trust
they come from
our Father's
loving hand

to believe
does not mean
to understand

can we
after our prayes
of sorrow
of bitterness
of despair

during our time of grief
during our time of mourning
in our suffering

believe

and act

then we become
light in the darkness
then we become Christ

then we can pray
with Saint Francis

Lord
make me an instrument
of thy peace

where there is hatred, let me sow love
where there is injury, pardon
where there is doubt, faith
where there is despair, hope
where there is darkness, light
and where there is sadness, joy

O Divine Master
grant that I may not so much
seek to be consoled, as to console
to be understood, as to understand
to be loved, as to love

for it is in giving
that we receive

it is in pardoning
that we are pardoned

and it is in dying
that we are born to eternal life

CONCLUSION

it was Christ's task
to reveal the Father's
tender loving kindness
and this he did
in word and deed

it was Christ who
spoke of the Father
and his love for man

it was Christ who
spoke of the Spirit—
he would not leave
us orphans

it was Christ who said
if we would ask
he and the Father
with the Spirit
would make their
home in us.

it was Christ who
promised us
waters of eternal life

as God's people
we are to be a sign to the world
of God's steadfast love

as Christ's friend
we are to continue
his word and work

our task is to show—
God loves all men—
he does not hate them

the Old Testament is a
slow unwinding
a slow unfolding of God's plan
man's seeking to know God
God revealing himself to man

in Christ, we have
the Father's clearest proof
of his love for man
and in the Spirit
we have the Father's
continuing pledge of
his love for man

in history
it is through Mary
that God became man

God's Mother

as the closing
of crocus
in early evening

so in his mother's
life hid—
only questions

have we of her
and a
song of praise

and deeds as
petals falling

as for the memory
the blood running

did she know

past her imagining
were the
deaths he'd suffer

to the uprise of
Easter to
make us laugh

full mightily with
the burst
of birdsong and

the leap of squirrels
to join
in his ever springing

ADULT DISCUSSION SERIES

ADULT DISCUSSION SERIES

WEEK 1
THE SACRAMENT OF ADVENT

WEEK 2
CHRIST HAS COME

WEEK 3
CHRIST COMES TODAY

WEEK 4
CHRIST'S FINAL COMING

Gary Giombi, Milwaukee Office of Religious Education

The Sacrament of Advent is an adult discussion series to be used in small groups in the parish during Advent. Groups meet once a week to talk and pray around a particular theme. These groups can meet in the home or in the parish. Participants should remain in the same group during the course of the program.

The format of the program consists of a series of reflection questions built around the week's theme, followed by a prayer service. A leader is needed for each meeting. It is suggested that a different person serve in this capacity for each meeting. Leaders should be chosen at least a week in advance so that they will have sufficient time to prepare for the session. The themes for the four weeks of Advent are:

1. The Sacrament of Advent
2. Christ Has Come
3. Christ Comes Today
4. Christ's Final Coming

The purpose of this program is to create an atmosphere in which participants can pray and reflect on the meaning of Advent as it unfolds in a particular week's theme. The leaders in particular should be aware of this goal and assist the group in focusing its attention on this mutual sharing. The following is one possible way of structuring the weekly meetings:

1. The leader presents a brief introduction to the theme.
2. Participants individually answer reflection questions. (Pencils and paper should be provided and a time limit announced when this begins.)

3. Group shares their responses to reflection questions.
4. Leader conducts the prayer service.
5. Any preparation for the following week's meeting, including follow-up activities, is discussed.

WEEK 1
THE SACRAMENT
OF ADVENT

The Lord will come again in glory at the fullness of time. Then he will take the whole universe, which he has been slowly perfecting through our hands, unite it to himself, and return it as a perfect gift to the Father. The universe will be transformed into a new creation in which God will be "all in all." The whole universe will be one peaceful city, a New Jerusalem that is completely filled with God's presence. And then God himself will feed us with living bread from the tree of eternal life.

Questions for Reflection

1. What are some of the "sacraments" of your life, occasions where you have been touched by the Lord? What was he calling you to? How did you respond?
2. Advent is a time of waiting. We await not only the Lord's final coming, but also a deepening of his coming into our heart and a deeper

appreciation of his coming in the life of Jesus. What have been some of your experiences of waiting? Have any had a religious dimension to them? Has your prayer ever been an experience of waiting? What is it like to have to wait?

3. Christ is bread and we are bread. How does Christ nourish you? How do other people nourish you? How do you nourish them?

4. God's presence is the greatest of his presents. What does this tell you about Christmas gift-giving? How do you give people the wonderful gift of your presence?

Many centuries ago, in a series of homilies St. Bernard described Advent as a sacrament. Of course, Advent isn't one of the *Seven Sacraments*. St. Bernard had in mind a wider and deeper meaning of the word sacrament: a depth encounter with the Lord. The many sacraments of our life celebrate the Lord's continuing presence to us, how he touches us and how we respond to him. Advent is a special "sacrament" which reminds us that we experience the Lord's presence in three aspects. He has already been present. He is present now. He is coming to be present with us in an even deeper way.

Two thousand years ago God became present to us in the person of Jesus, the son of Mary. At the fullness of time "the Word became flesh and dwelt among us." God touched human flesh and found a home there. Born in Bethlehem, the "city of bread," he came to be our nourishment.

The Lord continues to come to us today, not just in the *Seven Sacraments*, but in the thousand ways he daily touches our life he comes to dwell at the center of our heart, to transform us into himself. Every time we answer his call to respond lovingly to each person and event of our life, he is born again within us. We carry the pearl of great price, the hidden presence of the Lord, growing within us. He comes today, not just to one city, but to every city that has a heart to receive him. He still comes as our bread, nourishing us and calling us to become bread for others.

5. Make a list of all the people you have seen today, and briefly write what kind of an interchange you had with them. Reflect: Were you sacrament for them, an occasion of the Advent of the Lord into their life?
6. Read the Emmaus story (Lk 24:13-35). This is an account of various ways our life is sacrament, various opportunities we have for meeting the Lord (such as sorrow, persons, Scripture, etc.). How many can you find in the account?

Prayer Service

1. The leader calls the group to prayer.
2. The three readings for the First Sunday of Advent are read aloud.
3. There are ten minutes of silent prayer.
4. Each person in the group writes a short prayer beginning, "Lord, I am waiting for you to come into my life more deeply." The completed prayer is folded and put on a plate with the rest. Then people take them at random. Each person reads a prayer to the group.
5. End with the Lord's Prayer.

Follow-Up Activities (*Optional*)
1. Following the prayer service, be a sacrament by going up and talking to someone in the group whom you don't know.
2. During the week, bake some bread to be shared at the following week's prayer service.

WEEK 2
CHRIST
HAS
COME

In the beginning the Spirit of God brooded over the waters of chaos. Life emerged to fill the earth. At the fullness of time the Spirit of God brooded over the virgin Mary. She said "yes" to God, and God's own life became a human being.

When "the Word became flesh and dwelt among us," the years of waiting for a savior were fulfilled. This was God's Great Advent. He touched his creation by becoming a human being like us. In Jesus we meet God, and he touches us. Jesus is the great Advent sacrament from which all other sacraments flow.

A woman stands at the center of the great mystery of the Incarnation. The Blessed Mother, by her openness and receptivity to the Word of God,

creates the conditions necessary for his most
profound Advent into our world. In her own life
she recapitulates all the Advent themes.

Advent is a time of waiting for the Lord. Mary, as a
faithful Jewish woman, longed for the fulfillment
of the promises God had made to Israel. And
when God invited her to be a part of their
fulfillment, she waited long months nurturing the
child within her body.

Advent is a time of preparation to meet the Lord.
Mary's preparation was to keep herself open for
whatever God would ask of her. Her emptiness
became the womb that could be filled with the
seed of God's own life. When Carryll Houselander
described Mary as the "Reed of God," she was
pointing out that Mary was so open to God that
his own life giving breath, his own Spirit, could
breathe through her. She was God's musical
instrument that sang a beautiful song called the
Word made flesh.

Advent is also the season that celebrates the
victory of the power of light over the forces of
darkness. Mary was the woman of light, bearing
Jesus the "Light of the World" who was to become
a "Light of revelation to the gentiles." Her faith
was the light that allowed God's light to shine
forth.

Advent is a time of faith. We believe that the Lord
has come, is coming, and will come again. This is a
living faith that directs our whole life toward God.
Mary exemplifies this faith. Her "yes" teaches us

the power of our faith. When we say "yes" to God, we can change the world. Not only can faith move mountains, but, more remarkable still, it can make God present in the world.

Because Mary lived the Advent themes so well, she became the Ark of the Covenant. In Old Testament times, the Ark of the Covenant was a place of God's special presence. It carried the tablets of the ten commandments, some manna, and Aaron's shepherd staff. Mary became the place of God's most intense presence on earth. In her own womb she carried Jesus, the embodiment of the New Covenant between God and the human race. She bore our bread of life and Good Shepherd who will nourish and lead us, even as he did Mary, if we live her emptiness and faith.

Reflection Questions
1. How is your Advent this year a time of waiting, preparation, light, and faith?
2. How is your life, like Mary's, one of emptiness and receptivity, waiting for the coming of the Lord? How are you a person of faith?
3. What are some of the deeper meanings of "mother" and "virgin"? How are you called to be both? How do you live this out in your life?
4. How are you an Ark of the Covenant? What are some other Old Testament phrases that can be applied both to the Blessed Mother and to ourselves?
5. Is the Blessed Mother really relevant and important for the Church today? How? For you personally? How?
6. Read Matthew or Luke's infancy narratives. They tell how different people responded to God's

presence coming into their midst. Draw a
symbol for each person, and under it a word to
describe that response.
7. Write ten words that come to your mind in
response to the word "mother." Write ten that
come to your mind in response to the word
"virgin."
8. Immediately before the prayer service, someone
sets a loud timer (for under ten minutes). All
wait in silence for it to ring. Then play the song
"Dear Father" from the *Jonathan Livingston
Seagull* album.

Prayer Service

1. The leader calls the group to prayer.
2. The three readings for the Second Sunday of
Advent are read aloud.
3. There are ten minutes of silent prayer.
4. Each person in the groups writes a short prayer
beginning, "Lord, I am empty." Those who
wish, read them to the group.
5. Because our hands or arms are empty, we can
greet or embrace each other. The people
extend to each other some sign of greeting and
acceptance.
6. End with the Lord's Prayer.
7. If bread has been baked for this meeting, share
it among the group.

Follow-Up Activities (*Optional*)

1. During the week, make a cup or container out
of clay. Put it in a prominent place in your
home during the remainder of Advent. When
you look at it, take a few moments to reflect on
it as a symbol of emptiness and receptivity.

WEEK 3
CHRIST
COMES
TODAY

Our life is filled with sacrament and with Advent.
God is present to us, touching us, in every person
and event of our life. He is ever coming to meet
us, but he is also found within us. He dwells in the
depths of our heart, making each of us, like Mary,
an Ark of the Covenant.

When we lovingly respond to the Lord coming to
us in the persons and events of our life, his
presence within us deepens. We begin to become
transformed. When we, like Mary, empty ourselves
and open ourselves up to God in faith, Jesus is
born in the depths of our heart. We begin to
become Jesus, another advent of God into the
world. We are reborn as "another Christ."

This does not merely mean that we become "like
Christ." The mystery is far deeper than this. We do
not just behave as Jesus would behave. We are
changed at the center of our personality, the core
of our being. Jesus' attitudes slowly become our
attitudes. We become a "new creation," a new
presence of the Risen Lord in the world. Then we
can say with St. Paul, "I live now, not I, but Christ
lives in me."

The advent and birth of Jesus within us is not
without pain. We have to be broken and die so

that Jesus can be born. Our selfishness, our fear of being fully alive and human, our hesitation to receive and give love, our egocentric tendency to make ourselves the center from which we judge all things, these all must die so that we may be transformed into Jesus.

When we become another Christ, we will easily and spontaneously live his attitudes, do what he would do. Then our mind shall become his mind; our heart, his heart; our hands, his hands. Jesus will truly be born within us; his resurrection Spirit will have caught root in our heart.

The Christmas we celebrate each year is not primarily a remembrance of the first Christmas. It is a celebration of the ongoing advent and Christmas within our heart. We are celebrating our transformation into Christ. The manger is our heart. The babe that is being born is our new Christ-self.

Reflection Questions

1. How is Baptism an expression of our transformation into Christ?
2. How is the concept of "sanctifying grace" another way of describing our Christification?
3. How are we made in the image and likeness of God?
4. How do you experience God present in the people and events of your life? Give some examples.
5. What in particular in you has to die before Jesus can be born within you?
6. Can you think of examples of times when you

easily and spontaneously responded to a
situation as Christ would?

7. Can you find some hints in your life that Jesus
has taken root in your heart and is transforming
you into himself?

8. Find some Scripture quotes amplifying the idea
of our transformation into Christ.

9. List people who are "other Christs." If you can,
give an example from their lives which shows
this.

Prayer Service

1. The leader calls the group to prayer.

2. The three readings for the Third Sunday of
Advent are read aloud.

3. There are ten minutes of silent prayer.

4. Each person takes a small piece of paper and
writes something about himself or herself that
needs to be transformed. Then the papers are
folded, collected, and burned together.

5. The people pass a candle one to another saying,
"You are another Christ. You are a light to the
world." The ones to whom this is said cup their
hands over the flame. Then they put their hands
over their eyes, receiving the light and warmth.
Finally they take the candle and present it to the
person next to them.

6. End with the Lord's Prayer.

Follow-Up Activities (*Optional*)

1. Plant some seeds in a small pot. Take time to
care for them and watch them grow.

2. Find pictures of people encountering each
other in various ways. Create stories around
them, and share them with your family during
the week.

WEEK 4
CHRIST'S
FINAL
COMING

"Come, Lord Jesus, come quickly" the early Church prayed, longing for Jesus' return to establish his kingdom of peace and love. Two thousand years later, we still await this event, but realize that we are involved in hastening its approach. The sooner Christ is reborn within each of us, the sooner he can bring creation to its fullness.

Today we speak of the final coming of the Lord as bringing the world to completion rather than to destruction. When God created, he called everything "good." How could he destroy that which he found good? He will not destroy creation, but rather bring out the depths of the goodness and beauty that have so often been obscured by our sinful use of it. That "the Word became flesh" teaches us that at its core, the world is very good.

The epistles of St. Paul present Christ in his final coming as bringing a transformed creation, united with himself, to the Father as gift. When Christ came in his first two advents, he came only to people. He became flesh through the Blessed Mother and continues to become flesh through us. In his final coming he will take up all of creation as his flesh. Then, as St. Paul writes, "God will be all in all."

The Book of Revelation uses the image of the New Jerusalem to represent the transformed universe. The old Jerusalem was the holy city of God because of God's special presence in the temple. The New Jerusalem, the Book of Revelation tells us, will have no temple because God shall permeate the whole city, present in every single atom. The New Jerusalem will need no sun or moon or light because the brilliance of God's glorious presence will fill every corner.

This is a beautiful vision of what our world can become, a place where everyone and everything is sacrament, where everyone and everything carries the radiant presence of God.

This is already beginning to happen now, today. God is already transforming the world into the New Jerusalem through our very hands. As co-creators with God, our Christ-filled lives are helping to build the earth and bring creation to fullness. St. Paul described creation as groaning for fulfillment. We, as it were, hear that groaning and try to respond to it as best we can in our own unique way. Our very lives become the cry of "Come, Lord Jesus" that helps establish the New Jerusalem.

Reflection Questions

1. What were you taught about the "end of the world"? How does this compare with the "transformation of the world"?
2. What are some ways that your own life is helping to build the earth, to bring about the New Jerusalem?

3. Gregory Baum writes that believing in God is believing that tomorrow can be different from today. How would you like your life and your world to be better tomorrow? What can you do about it?
4. Who are some people today who are helping transform the world into the New Jerusalem?
5. How is saying that God will be "all in all" different from pantheism?
6. Find quotes from St. Paul about the New Creation. Find the Book of Revelation's description of the New Jerusalem.

Prayer Service

1. The leader calls the group to prayer.
2. The three readings of the Fourth Sunday of Advent are read aloud.
3. There are ten minutes of silent prayer.
4. Each person in the group writes a short prayer of petition and puts it in a chalice. Then each person takes one and reads it.
5. Each person takes a cup with a very small amount of wine in it. Then each person pours their wine into the chalice, saying aloud some blessings that the Lord has given them. Finally all share the chalice.
6. End with the Lord's Prayer.

Optional Activity

This exercise can be done after the sharing session and before the prayer service. Be sure to have participants bring the following materials:

- white paper (6' × 12')
- old magazines
- paste and scissors

- crayons or drawing chalk
- cardboard boxes
- strings of flashing Christmas tree lights
- aluminum foil

1. Fasten a large sheet of white paper to a wall (at least 6' × 12'. Print shops often give them away, left-overs from billboard pictures). Have the group draw a mural of the New Jerusalem coming into being.
2. On a similar piece of paper everyone pastes magazine pictures of things they like. Then all label them "good."
3. People cut out pictures of what they would like the New Jerusalem to be like. Then they paste them to boxes, and fasten the boxes together for their city.
4. Line a medium size cardboard box (12" square) with a string of 6 or 8 independently flashing Christmas tree lights. Then cover all the insides but the bulbs with wrinkled aluminum foil. Turn on the lights and see a beautiful display, the New Jerusalem, the city of light.

ADVENT/CHRISTMAS AT
HOME

CELEBRATING ADVENT AND CHRISTMAS AT HOME

Kathleen Grusky Connolly

Introduction

When we think of customs that are important to us, we realize that we first learned them in our homes as children. In various areas of our lives, our families have passed on to us many traditions that we now cherish. Some of them, like turkey on Thanksgiving, we share with many other people. Some of them are unique to our ethnic group, region or household. But they are all rich with meaning.

The Advent season presents us with both temptation and a graced opportunity. The temptation is to prepare for Christmas as the world does, concentrating on the material aspect of Christmas and its place in our own little world. The grace we are offered in Advent is to prepare for the coming of Christ, to journey with the Church toward the stable in Bethlehem and all it symbolizes. In doing so, we reach out beyond ourselves to the larger community, and in the process share with our families a heritage whose value cannot be measured in money.

This section focuses on celebrating Advent and Christmas at home with your immediate family and extended family. The ideas offered here by no means exhaust the possibilities. Rather, they form a base on which you and your family can build an

Advent/Christmas tradition that is rich in meaning for you. These suggestions for prayer, celebration and activity have two goals: building community (both within the family and beyond the family) and helping them become more aware of and open to the many ways in which Jesus comes into our lives.

Each topic within this section—from Advent wreaths to making eggnog—lends itself to family sharing and activity that can become a part of your family Advent/Christmas tradition. You are encouraged to use the activities as they are or adapt them for the particular needs of your family.

Isaiah prophesied that the people who walked in darkness have seen a great light (9:1). It is hoped that this section will help you and your family to walk through Advent renewed by the light that Christ brings to humanity.

ADVENT WREATH

The Advent wreath has long been a way of focusing our attention on the coming of Christ, the light of the world. Making a wreath, having a simple ceremony for the lighting of each candle are ways in which family members (and friends) can share in the preparation for Christmas.

Making a Wreath: Wreaths can be bought, but of course it is more fun and more satisfying to make one yourself. The wreath should be bought or made so that it is all ready in time for the first Sunday of Advent.

The basic materials you need to make a wreath are: a base, a large quantity of evergreen twigs, 4 candles (3 purple and 1 pink, about 6″ × 8″ in height), and purple ribbon. Nails or hat pins can be used to secure the candles, depending on the type base you use.

One type of base that is easy to make is made of styrofoam. An arts and crafts store will have a selection of circular styrofoam pieces from which to choose. On the base, draw four evenly-spaced circles where the candles will be placed. With a knife, cut the spaces for the candles. Insert the candles and secure them with hat pins. The evergreen twigs are then wrapped around the base of each candle, and all around the wreath. The ribbon is used to decorate the wreath.

Newspaper can also be used to make the wreath base. For this base, you will also need some stiff wire (an old hanger will do) and some fine wire and nails. Use the heavy wire to form a circle of the size you want for your wreath. Wrap newspaper around the wire frame and secure it with the fine wire. Be generous with both newspaper and wire. When you are finished, soak the frame in water, thoroughly saturating the newspaper. This helps to keep the twigs fresh. Now tie the twigs around the frame, using fine wire. Secure this wire to the wire holding the newspaper together. When the frame is covered, insert 4 nails into the frame at equal intervals. The nails should be long and extend about one inch above the wreath. Then wrap the ribbon around the wreath. Remove the nails and heat them, inserting into the bottom of each candle to make a small hole. Now place the nails back into the wreath and fit the candles into place.

Wreaths may be hung; however, it is probably better to keep your wreath in a place where all can see it. The table where the family usually eats is often an ideal place. When making and displaying the wreath, be sure that younger children are included in the project as much as possible. Although small children should not be handling sharp objects, there are other things that they can do. They can assist in purchasing material for the wreath, and, with the guidance of adults or older children, can help in working with the twigs and ribbon. Their participation, no matter how limited because of age or ability, helps them to feel more a part of the project.

Now that your wreath is made, what next? One candle of the wreath is lit each week, along with any candles that have been lit the previous week. The pink candle is lit on the Third Sunday of Advent, Gaudete Sunday, and is a special symbol of joy. It is a good idea to plan your candle-lighting ceremony for the same day each week, perhaps after the family meal for that day. Family members should be encouraged to set this time aside and not make other plans unless unforeseen circumstances arise.

The Candle Ceremony: The following is a brief rite for the family to use each week in lighting the Advent wreath. You may add to it by including such elements as a reading of the Scripture from the Sunday liturgy of the week, additional singing or discussion. Whatever you do, it is good to have a definite end to the ceremony. Without this, people (especially children) can become restive thinking of "When will we be finished?" One possibility is to plan the ceremony after a meal but before dessert.

Preparation: Have the Advent wreath in the center of the table. Each week a different person should be chosen to light the candle(s). It might be well to have an adult do so the first week, when the children may feel unsure of what is going to happen. Before beginning, ask everyone to be quiet for a few moments and collect themselves. If possible, have the family learn "Advent Song" (*Dandelions*, Mary Lu Walker, Paulist Press). This song has a verse for the lighting of each candle.

First Week of Advent

Theme: "Stay awake, for the time is coming."

The leader reads the theme aloud, and the family discusses the following questions. (Again, make sure to encourage the younger children to take part—they probably have plenty to say!)
What kinds of events make us want to stay awake, even when we're tired?
What does "awake" mean? Is it just avoiding sleep, or is more involved?
The time mentioned means the birth of Jesus. How can we be "awake" for this?

Leader:
Father, we thank you for sending us your Son

Jesus. We ask you to help us to remember, at this busy time, what Christmas means. Awaken us to your presence in our lives. We make this prayer through Jesus, your Son and our brother.

All:
Amen.

The leader lights one purple candle.

All:
Sing verse 1 and chorus of "Advent Song."
Dessert is served. The candle is extinguished when all are through eating.

Second Week of Advent

Theme: "A voice cries in the wilderness: 'Prepare a way for the Lord.' "

Questions:
How can we as a family prepare for the Lord's coming?
How can we prepare as individuals?
What can I do this week to make someone else's Christmas preparation more meaningful?

Leader:
Father, this Christmas season demands much physical preparation. Help us not to lose sight of the ways we can prepare in our hearts to celebrate Christmas. We make this prayer in Jesus' name.

All:
Amen.

The leader lights a new purple candle, pauses, then lights the candle that burned the previous week.

All:

Sing verse 2 and chorus of "Advent Song." End as in week one.

Third Week in Advent

Theme: "My soul rejoices in the Lord."

Questions:

What do we as a family have to rejoice about? Do I take time to stop and praise God for his goodness?

Who are the people around us whose rejoicing has been silenced by death, sickness, poverty, hardship? What can we do to bring an element of joyfulness into their lives?

Leader:

Father, we praise you for all that you are and all that you've given to us. Help us to be people who share our joy with all whom we meet. We ask this through Jesus Christ our Lord.

All:

Amen.

The leader lights the pink candle, pauses and then lights the candles from weeks one and two.

All:

Sing verse 3 and chorus of "Advent Song." End as week one.

Fourth Sunday of Advent

Theme: "He will be called Emmanuel, which means God-with-us."

Questions:
When do I feel God's presence most strongly?
When am I least aware of it?
What does it mean to me when I think that God loved us so much he became one of us?
How can I bring the presence of God to others?

Leader:
Father, as we draw close to Christmas, we stop and realize how much you love us in sending your only Son to live among us as one of us. You send your Spirit to guide us. Help us to stay near to you and to help others to be near you also. We ask you this in the name of Jesus, God-with-us.

All:
Amen.
The leader lights the one candle that has not burned, pauses, lights the pink candle, then the candles from weeks one and two.

All:
Sing verse 4 and chorus of "Advent Song."
End as in previous weeks.

You might wish to choose one other night during the week as a time to say a special grace before the evening meal and sing the appropriate verse and chorus of the "Advent Song."

The Advent wreath ceremony is designed as a family event, but there is no reason why others outside the family cannot join in. You may know an elderly couple whose children live far away or a person who lives alone whom you might invite to share in your Advent ceremony. While it may not be feasible to have guests for dinner every week, others outside the family could be invited over after the meal and share in dessert with the family.

ADVENT CALENDAR

Right after Thanksgiving, the Christmas countdown begins. The number of days left until Christmas is always mentioned in conjunction with the time we have left for shopping. Of course, there are many other ways in which to prepare for Christmas that go deeper than trips to the shopping center. One way to help ourselves to prepare for Christmas in this deeper way is to make and use an Advent calendar.

The Advent calendar, like the Advent wreath, may be bought rather than made (see Bibliography). However, making an Advent calendar is a project in which the whole family can take part. Your own unique calendar will also personalize the way in which your family prepares for the birth of Christ.

To make a calendar, you can use a ready-made calendar for the month of December, filling in the boxes for the different days. The larger the calendar, the better, because a large calendar affords more space for drawing and printing. If you wish to start from scratch, you can get a large piece of drawing paper, oak tag or matte board from an art supply store. On it, draw boxes for the days of the month of December, but do not number them.

Whether you are using a printed calendar or one you have drawn yourself, you will need to make little "doors" for each of the twenty-four days preceding Christmas. On the front of each door, mark the date. These doors are then glued to the calendar so that they can be opened each day. Behind the door, you can draw figures, write quotes from Scripture, a thought for the day, or any number of other things. Some ideas are listed below.

People and Places of Christmas: In the boxes behind the doors, family members can draw representations of people and places associated with the Advent and Christmas seasons. If you have old Christmas cards or catalogues, pictures can be cut out and pasted. Some days of the month particularly lend themselves to this. (See section of "December Saints" below.)

Scripture quotes: Each day can have a reference to a quote from Scripture, taken perhaps from one of the readings of the day. "We meet Jesus in . . ." Each box can contain a picture or name of a person (family member, friend, acquaintance) or event in which we meet Jesus. Be imaginative! These could include simple things (the sunrise, the family eating together), people who are of significance to the family or a family member, events that are special to the family. One final note here: people whose birthdays fall near Christmas often feel "cheated" because their special day is overshadowed by holiday preparations. If you have a December birthday in your family, make sure it becomes part of your celebration.

Now that your calendar is made, what do you do with it? Like the Advent wreath, the calendar should be displayed in a place where all have access to it. This may mean hanging it at a point lower than adult eye level, so that little children can see it without difficulty. Try to open the door for the day when the family is all together. This might be at breakfast, though for many families breakfast is an "eat and run" affair. You might find it profitable to open the door of the next day at dinner of the night before.

Depending on what you have put on your Advent calendar, different activities can take place. Scripture quotes can be read and reflected on or discussed. Someone might open a door ahead of time and prepare a little explanation of the figure or place found there. However you use your calendar, remember that children (and adults too!) dislike homework. Whatever activities you design to go with your calendar, please keep two things in mind.

1. Simple activities enable younger children to enter more fully into the family preparations.
2. Everyone feels rushed and overtaxed during this season. The purpose of the calendar is to create a time and space for relaxation and sharing.

Avoid projects that might be seen as more work, and therefore done poorly, or not done at all.

THE ADVENT GAME
Mr. Gary Giombi, Milwaukee Office of Religious Ed.

During Advent, each evening at supper a stack of envelopes is brought to the table. There is an envelope marked for each day of Advent, special for that day. Everyone waits through the meal, eager to find out what will be in the evening's envelope. When the meal is finished, one of the members of the family opens the envelope and reads it to the family (or someone else reads it if the child is too small). Everyone, including the parents, takes a turn one day or another.

What Is in the Envelopes?

There is a great variety of possibilities here. The envelope may contain something to show or read, like a beautiful picture to be posted on the bulletin board, or pictures to be used the next day as placemats. It may be a poem or short story or song. It may be an interesting little piece of family history to remember and enjoy together. It could be a prayer.

Or the envelope may contain something to do. This could be directed just toward the person opening the envelope. "Whoever opens this envelope gets to choose what the family will do together this evening," or even, shudder, "what the family will watch on TV this evening." Or

"Whoever opens this envelope gets to choose
Mom or Dad to do the dishes for them next time
their turn comes up." Or "Whoever opens this
envelope gets to do the dishes tonight." Or
"Whoever opens this envelope gets to make a
decoration for the Christmas tree tonight." The
possibilities are almost limitless. Because the
envelopes may sometimes (rarely) contain some
extra work for the opener, it becomes a little risky
and thus more exciting.

The envelope could contain something for the
whole family to do. "Everyone will work together
on the supper tomorrow night." "Everyone will
receive two dollars to spend at . . ." "Everyone will
take five minutes now to pray silently together."
"Everyone will help make a Christmas wreath that
we will hang up this evening."

How are the contents of the envelopes
determined? The parents could write them all out
themselves. But then it would not be so much of a
family project, and the parents themselves would
miss out on the excitement because they would
know what was in each envelope. Perhaps a better
way might be to have the parents or older children
write the notes that are for the special days (see
below). For the other days, everyone writes notes,
perhaps the younger children helped by the older
ones. Then the notes are randomly put into the
envelopes that do not get a special feast note. This
way no one, not even the parents, knows what is
in all of the envelopes.

The following is a list of some of the special feasts

of Advent, with some ideas that could be amplified in the notes:

Nov. 30: St. Andrew—An Apostle

Dec. 3: St. Francis Xavier—A great missionary

Dec. 6: St. Nicholas—Stockings hung up or shoes placed outside on the eve

Dec. 8: Immaculate Conception—Our congenital weakness in loving

Dec. 8: The Enlightenment of the Buddha—Candles, meditation

Dec. 13: St. Lucy—Candles and sweet rolls

Dec. 14: St. John of the Cross—Great prayerful person and reformer

Dec. 17-24: "O Antiphons"—Jesus is Wisdom, Lord, Root of Jesse, Key of David, Rising Sun, King of the Nations, and God-With-Us

Dec. 21: Winter Solstice—Shortest day of the year, feast of the unconquered sun

Dec. 21: St. Thomas—Doubt and faith

First Sunday of Advent: "Stir up Sunday"—Christmas pudding

All Sundays of Advent: Use of the readings

Variable: Hanukkah—Jewish feast of the Lights

The following is a list of words and phrases that may trigger in you some ideas for the envelopes:

Waiting—song from *Jonathan Livingston Seagull*

Presence

Advent Wreath

Christmas Tree—buy or cut, and decorate

Tree of paradise

Crack nuts through Advent to use in Christmas coffee cake

"Come Lord Jesus, come quickly"—*Maranatha*

Family tree—Jesse tree—*Roots*

Kristkindl—choosing a name of a secret family
member to be specially nice to

Self-discipline—gentle fasting or abstinence

Decorations of every sort

John the Baptist—"Prepare Ye the Way of the
Lord"—*Godspell*

Isaiah the Prophet

The Blessed Mother—openness, waiting,
emptiness, *Reed of God*

St. Joseph

Shepherds

Kings—each day, starting from a far room in the
house, move them closer to the crib

Emmanuel—"God with us" Christmas hymn

Bethlehem means House of Bread—bake bread
together

The crib and manger

Handel's *Messiah*

Midnight Mass

A new home-made Christmas tree decoration to
mark each year

Psalm 24

Making Christmas gifts together

Christmas meal—prepared all through Advent

Christmas cards—making and sending

Making Christmas candles and candles for
special feasts

The Star

Christmas carols

Advent journal

Yule log, on December 21

Poinsettia

Wassail drink or egg nog

Mistletoe and holly

Santa Claus

Piñata—Spanish and Mexican custom

Some Suggestions for Playing the Game

So, there you have the Advent game. Besides being a family fun activity, it builds traditions and fosters the Advent theme of waiting, both for each night's envelope and for Christmas when the stack of envelopes is exhausted. It draws the family together, not just when you play it during Advent, but even as you plan it before Advent begins. Perhaps Thanksgiving weekend would be a good time to gather together and write the various notes that will be in the envelopes. There are a multitude of Christmas books that can amplify my brief suggestions and offer many more.

Oh yes, if someone in your family doesn't want to play the game, don't force him or her. Just let them be present as the others play, and from time to time invite them to join in if they want. Perhaps they will be playing before Advent is over.

DECEMBER SAINTS

December 6, St. Nicholas

Not much is known about the person of St. Nicholas, the early Christian saint who evolved into the legend we know today as "Santa Claus." Nicholas was born in the late third century in Patara, part of present-day Turkey. He became Bishop of Myra, and his death date was fixed on December 6, 342. He was canonized by the ninth century, and the miracles attributed to him on behalf of children and others in need caused him to be known as a protector of the downtrodden.

How did St. Nicholas become Santa Claus? The evolution of one figure into the other has a long and complicated history. In 1969, the pope dropped St. Nicholas' day from the Roman Calendar and made celebration of his feast optional. If St. Nicholas, himself, has become more obscure as time goes on, the "person" we call Santa Claus has developed more with the passage of time.

As Western Europe became Christian, many pagan practices were kept but integrated with Christian feasts and given a Christian meaning. The mid-winter practice of exchanging gifts, pagan in origin, became associated with St. Martin (November 11) and St. Nicholas (December 6). Different practices involving these two saints developed in different countries in Western Europe. It was only natural that many of these customs came to the New World as Europeans began emigrating to America.

The image of Santa Claus as we have it now in America came to be established in the nineteenth century, and owes a lot to the writer Washington Irving. Irving's *A History of New York* (1809) makes several references to Santa Claus, his appearance and his habits, including gift-giving. However, the major alterations in details about Santa Claus came as a result of the work of two men: Clement Clarke Moore and Thomas Nast. Moore is credited with the authorship of the famous poem "The Night Before Christmas," which originally appeared anonymously as "An Account of a Visit from St. Nicholas" in the Troy (New York) *Sentinel* on December 23, 1823. The details the poem gives regarding Santa's appearance, habits and *modus operandi* became fixed in the popular imagination.

Thomas Nast, an illustrator for Harper's *Weekly*, ran a series of Christmas drawings for that publication during the years 1863-1866. Again, these drawings helped to establish what Santa looked like and what he did. The jolly old man who appears on Christmas Eve in a red suit is somewhat of a far cry from the saintly Bishop of Myra.

Finally, Santa Claus's existence became the topic of one of America's most widely known editorials. In 1897, young Virginia O'Hanlon wrote a letter to the *New York Sun*. At the age of eight, Virginia began to have doubts about the reality of Santa Claus, so she wrote to the paper asking for their opinion. On Sept. 21, 1897, the *Sun* published its answer in the form of an editorial: "Yes, Virginia, there is a Santa Claus."

Since the era of Moore, Nast and the *Sun* editorial, the only significant expansion of the Santa Claus legend has been the addition of another reindeer to his faithful crew. The story of Rudolph the Red-Nosed Reindeer was conceived for the Montgomery Ward store in 1939 as a promotional event. Ten years later he was immortalized in a song recorded by Gene Autry and the late Bing Crosby. It was a hit both here and in other countries.

Yes, Virginia, it certainly is a long trip from the feast day of a fourth century bishop to the popular lore surrounding the mythical Santa Claus. Your family may want to investigate this journey in more detail (see Bibliography). Despite the informational gaps in the story, one thing is certain: Santa Claus is here to stay.

December 8, Feast of the Immaculate Conception

The term "Immaculate Conception" means that Mary, by virtue of a unique grace, was free from original sin from the very beginning of her life, that is, from the moment of her conception. There is sometimes popular confusion between this doctrine and the teaching concerning Jesus' conception by the power of the Holy Spirit. Although the grace at her conception is related to Jesus in the sense that Mary receives this grace in view of her future merit, it is important to keep in mind the distinction between Mary's conception and that of her Son.

The teaching regarding Mary's conception is not found explicitly in Scripture, but seems to have arisen from the application of the general teaching regarding Mary's holiness. In that sense it is part of the apostolic teaching. Historically, this teaching was open to discussion within the Church, but as time went on, the popes more strongly defended the position of those who supported the teaching. In 1846, the Sixth Provincial Council of Baltimore named the Immaculate Conception the patron feast of the United States. Pope Pius IX defined this teaching as a dogma of the Church in 1854. That same year, he stated and explained the dogma in the encyclical *Ineffabilis Deus*.

Unfortunately, our first association with this feast

may be the thought that it is a holyday of obligation, or a day off for parochial school students. The fact that the Church has defined this dogma, and calls us to celebrate the Eucharist on this feast day, tells us to look beyond the "externals" and consider the importance of Mary in the life of Christians. How can we do this as a family during the Advent/Christmas season?

Mary is certainly a prominent figure in the Christmas story. Her feast day, falling as it does during Advent, presents a good opportunity to talk about Mary and her example to us. The example of Mary focuses on two important aspects of faith: the internal or personal element of responding to God's word, and the external or communal element of responding in service to others.

Either on the eve of this feast, or that evening when the family is together, it might be helpful to spend a little time talking about Mary. Younger children may have questions about what this feast means and why it is important. It would be good to share the reading for this feast day (Lk 1:26-38) and discuss what happens in the account.
—How would I have felt if I were Mary?
—Think of the times you were asked to do something important. How did you feel? Scared?

Important? Confused? Happy?
—We honor Mary because of her desire to do God's will, even if that seemed difficult to her. In my own life, what things do I find difficult that I would like to say "yes" to? How does the example of Mary help me?

December 13, St. Lucy

Like St. Nicholas, St. Lucy is a "Christmas saint" about whom little is known. She was born in Sicily and according to legend gave her dowry money to the poor when she was a young girl. This was considered quite peculiar, and she was burned as a witch in the early fourth century. St. Lucy's greatest popularity today is in Sweden. According to tradition, she helped the Swedish people during a time of famine.

It is customary in Sweden for the oldest daughter in a family to give family members "St. Lucy buns" on the morning of the saint's feast. Young girls dress up as "Lucy brides," wearing long white gowns and a wreath in their hair made of candles and greenery. They often sing "Santa Lucia" while serving the cakes.

Your family may wish to incorporate some aspects of St. Lucy Day into your celebration of Advent. Depending on the variety of bakeries in your neighborhood, you may be able to purchase Saint Lucy buns. Or you may wish to make the buns yourself beforehand. This is more time-consuming, but it can be done efficiently and involve all members of the family if jobs are divided up among you. A recipe is included here.

We have become somewhat more conscious today of the problem of world hunger and the need to share our resources with others. The St. Lucy legend incorporates the idea of sharing with those in need.

Your family might wish to examine ways in which this feast could be an occasion for sharing with others. Most parishes and neighborhood organizations offer means by which people can contribute food for a meal for those in need. You might also consider sharing a meal with an elderly friend or neighbor living on a fixed income. Have family members discuss in advance how they would like to observe this feast.

SIMPLIFIED LUCIA BUNS

If the traditional Lucia dough seems too troublesome and time-consuming, a basic sugar cookie dough may be satisfactorily used. This simplified version is adapted from Susan Purdy's book, *Christmas Decorations for You to Make.*

Materials
1 cup sweet butter or margarine
½ cup sugar
2½ cups sifted all-purpose flour
2 tablespoons vanilla extract or 1 tablespoon
  almond extract
Yellow food coloring

Method
1. Blend the sugar and butter and mix until fluffy.
2. Add vanilla or almond extract and several drops of yellow food coloring.
3. Add sifted flour, ½ cup at a time, mixing well. After you add all of the flour, mix with your hands.
4. Flour a pastry board. Take about ½ cup of dough at a time and roll it into narrow strips

about ⅜-inch thick. Form into Lucia shapes and put on greased cookie sheets using a floured spatula. Keep them at least an inch apart so that the cookies will have room to spread.

5. Bake at 350° about 10 minutes or until golden brown. Cool. (If the dough cracks or breaks while forming into shapes pinch or pat it back together. When using dough made with real butter, warm the lumps in your hands to soften slightly before rolling out.)

6. If desired, dip raisins in a mixture of confectioner's sugar and water. Place for the features.

O ANTIPHONS

The "O Antiphons" are designed for use at Vespers before and after the Magnificat during the period from December 17 through December 23. The original melody is lost, but the antiphons are usually sung in Latin as a Gregorian chant. The themes of the antiphons are drawn from the Old Testament, largely from the prophet Isaiah. The basic pattern of the antiphons is the title followed by statements of praise and petition related to the title. Following are the titles of the "O Antiphons" and a brief explanation of each.

Sapientia: Wisdom, the Word of God. We pray that God will show us his wisdom.

Adonai: My Lord. This was a title used to address God when the sacred name YHWH was not spoken. It refers to God in an intimate way as the ruler of his people.

Radix: Root of Jesse. Jesse was the father of David and therefore an ancestor of Jesus. This is a reference to the prophecy that the Messiah would be a descendant of Jesse (Is 11).

Clavis: Key of David. Keys are a symbol of power and authority. Jesus is heir to the keys of David.

Oriens: This title is more difficult to translate than the others. The basic idea is dawn or rising sun. Here we are praying for enlightenment for all people.

Rex: King of nations. Here the Messiah is invoked as king of all people, the one who will unite both Jews and Gentiles.

Emmanuel: God-with-us. Isaiah, in chapter 7, prophesies the birth of a son to the virgin, the son to be called Emmanuel. This title has a sense of immediacy—God-*with-us*.

Activities related to the "O Antiphons":
If you have made an Advent calendar, these titles could be entered in the box for the appropriate day. The titles could then be the focus of that day's prayer and/or discussion. If you are making decorations for your tree, these titles yield good symbols that could be designed and executed for decorations.

The most obvious activity, and perhaps the most difficult, would be to attempt to sing the "O Antiphons" on the appropriate days. Consult your parish organist, a copy of a hymnal or *New Catholic World* (Nov/Dec 1975) for a musical arrangement. If anyone in the family is musically inclined, or if you have a piano, you might try to learn the melody, which is a simple chant. Those families who prefer not to sing the antiphons could recite them each day, in the pattern of antiphon-verse-antiphon.

When discussing the "O Antiphons" with your family, it is important to remember that while Latin and chants are familiar to parents, children probably have little knowledge of them. Even if your children are of college age, they are barely old enough to remember when Mass was celebrated in anything but English, and their experience of Church music is very different from that of chant.

This might be a good opportunity to share with them a little about some earlier Church traditions, and how and why they have changed. Adults today are a "bridge" generation between pre- and post-Vatican II practices. There is no finer gift you can give your children than a deeper knowledge and appreciation of their religious heritage.

THE CRECHE AND JESSE TREE

The creche is a central symbol for our celebration of Christ's coming at Christmas. The particulars of the creche your family displays depend upon such factors as available space, time, and personal style. Stables and figures can be purchased at many stores. You may wish to make your own creche, but this must be done far in advance of the holidays. You can make your own stable, and then buy figures for it. Figures, themselves, can be made by carving or by shaping the forms with play dough and then painting them. Creches can also be made using figures cut from Christmas cards, which are then mounted on cardboard stands. See the bibliography for books that give detailed instructions for assembling your own creche.

The creche should be put up sometime before Christmas, with the manger left empty until Christmas Day and the Magi somewhere outside the stable so that they look like they are en route to the stable (see section on Epiphany). The following prayer service is designed to accompany the assembly of the creche. When a date is decided for this event, it is marked on the Advent calendar. Like the other family Advent celebrations described here, all family members should be in attendance unless some last minute emergency arises.

Preparation: Stable should be set up in a prominent place without any of the figures in it. Each person is responsible for one of the following nativity figures (roles can be doubled or split, depending on family size):

Mary
Joseph
shepherds
animals
angel
Magi
Infant Jesus

The appropriate prayer is read, and the corresponding figure placed in its spot. The infant should be placed in the manger on Christmas Day.

Reader:

Mary, you said "yes" to God's call to give birth to and nurture his Son. Help us to seek God's will in our lives as you did in yours. Aid us in seeing Christ in all who come to us seeking love and growth. Let us pray for our mother, _____ and our grandmothers _____ and _____.

All:

Amen.

(Figure of Mary is placed to one side of the manger.)

Reader:

Joseph, you placed your faith in God and loved and cared for Jesus as your own son. Help us to make all who enter our home feel unity with us. Let us pray for our father _____ and our grandfathers _____ and _____.

All:

Amen.

(Figure of Joseph is placed to other side of manger.)

Reader:

The shepherds heard the good news of salvation and praised God. Like them, let us give glory to God for all he does for us.

All:

Amen.

(Shepherds are placed around stable.)

Reader:

Animals were Jesus' first companions after his

birth. Let us show reverence for all creation and use the fruits of the earth wisely.

All:
Amen.
(Animals are placed in stable.)

Reader:
The angel proclaimed the good news of Christ's birth. May we also proclaim the good news by the way we live and the care we show to others.

All:
Amen.
(Angel is placed at top of stable.)

Reader:
The Magi journeyed at great length to see Jesus and proclaim God's goodness. May our life journey be filled with faith and guided by God's light and wisdom.

All:
Amen.
(Magi are placed en route to stable.)
On Christmas Day:

Reader:
Today we celebrate the birth of Jesus, God become human to live among us. May we be signs of his continuing presence in the world.

All:
Amen.
(Infant is placed in manger.)
This service can conclude with the reading of the account of Jesus' birth, Luke 2:1-20.

Another popular Christmas tradition is the Jesse
tree. For information on making a Jesse tree, see
the section "Advent in the Classroom."

DECORATING AND BLESSING THE TREE

Christmas wouldn't be Christmas without a tree,
we are told, and certainly the tree is a focal point
of holiday festivities. Buying and decorating the
family tree are events everyone wants to take part
in, while taking down the tree (see below) is a
process which everyone would like to help with,
but. . . . Perhaps we are all reluctant to see
Christmas pass.

The origin of our custom of decorating a tree lies
in the mystery plays presented in Germany around
the fifth century. The tree was placed in the
middle of the Garden of Paradise, and symbolized
the coming of Christ. It was decorated with apples,
representing sin, and wafers symbolizing the
Blessed Sacrament. Later these wafers were
replaced by pastries cut into different shapes. The
popularity of the tree did not spread until the
nineteenth century, and in 1856, President Franklin
Pierce put up the first Christmas tree in the White
House.

Today people can choose between live and
artificial trees. Each have advantages and
disadvantages. Although buying a tree is fun, it can
become tedious, and depending on weather and
other factors, pickings can be slim. If you buy a
tree sometime in advance of Christmas, keep it
outdoors until you are ready to decorate it. A live

tree decorated a week or two before Christmas runs the risk of turning brown and losing many of its needles before Christmas Day. Make sure you have an adequate base for the tree, and keep it filled with water. A dry tree and the heat from Christmas lights can be a hazard. Check local ordinances regarding disposal of the tree. After all is said and done, the main advantage of a live tree is just that—it looks and smells like a real tree. Artificial trees have the advantage of needing less care. They can remain up as long as you want them up, and then are just stored away for use the following year. In choosing your tree, try to include all family members in the process.

Once you've acquired your tree, try to decorate it as close to Christmas as possible. Christmas Eve would be ideal, but is often impractical. Setting the tree up too far in advance anticipates the feast of Christmas and can make the tree almost another piece of furniture by the time the feast occurs. Decide on the day you're going to decorate your tree, and make sure family members will be home. If you have an Advent calendar, this is surely an event to be placed on it.

If your children are young, you may want to do the difficult work (setting up the tree, stringing lights) and let the children help with other things according to their age and ability. Decorations made at home or at school can be displayed prominently. Some families enjoy tree-trimming parties, at which guests are asked to bring a decoration as "admission," preferably a decoration they've made themselves or personalized in some way.

The trees we put up, like the trees of the German mystery plays, symbolize the coming of Christ. Blessing the tree helps keep this symbolism fresh in our minds. The following blessing can be said by a member of the family, either immediately before putting the decorations up, or after the tree has been completely dressed.

"Heavenly Father, this tree symbolizes the gifts of life and growth you've given to your creation. Soon this tree will be surrounded by the gifts we give to each other. Help us to be grateful for all you have given us, especially the gift of each other. We make this prayer through Jesus, your Son and the supreme gift of your love."

ETHNIC CUSTOMS

The celebration of Advent and Christmas around the world is as varied as there are countries. Listed here are but a few of the customs and traditions found in other countries. It would take an entire book to do justice to the topic, and indeed some have been written. Consult the bibliography for references for learning more about the observance of the holidays in other countries. As an Advent project, you might like to research the customs of the countries from which your ancestors came.

Mexico: The observance of Christmas south of our border in Mexico begins nine days before Christmas with *las posadas* (processions). Mary and Joseph were thought to have begun their journey to Bethlehem nine days before Christ's birth; hence, the beginning of the processions at that time. Some people take part in the processions as a family; some have nine families join together. If a family does this alone, the procession is inside their house; if it is a group of families, they visit the houses of each family. The participants are divided into two groups: travelers and hosts. The travelers march with candles and are led by children bearing replicas of Mary and Joseph. The hosts stand at each house (or each room of one house) and refuse Mary and Joseph admittance until they arrive at the last house (or room). There the travelers are allowed to enter, and an altar and nativity scene are set up. All say a prayer and then have a festive party featuring a piñata (see the section "Advent in the Classroom" for instructions on making your own piñata).

The nine days of celebration is also a theme in *Puerto Rico* where people attend a Mass of the Carols at 5:30 A.M. on each of the nine days. *Trullas* or carol singers travel about singing traditional songs and receiving food, drink, and, occasionally, money for their singing. The feeding of the *trullas* is a lavish—and costly—affair.

An old Spanish legend has it that the only time a rooster crowed at midnight was to announce the birth of Jesus. Therefore on Christmas Eve Puerto Ricans attend the Mass of the Rooster at midnight. After Mass, a statue of the infant is venerated. In most Latin American countries, gifts are exchanged at Epiphany.

In *Spain* itself a great celebration begins on the feast of the Immaculate Conception and lasts for a week. Christmas Day is a time for feasting and the exchanging of presents. Epiphany is an important day during which villagers take cake, fruit and straw and, accompanied by bells and horns, walk to the edge of the village to meet the three kings. Each year, the kings seem to have taken another route, and the children get to eat the treats prepared for the magi. When the villagers return to the village, the kings are in the village Church.

Another interesting Spanish custom is the *Ojo de Dios* (Eye of God). See the section "Advent in the Parish" for a description.

The star of Bethlehem figures prominently during Christmas time in *Poland*. The first star to appear in the sky on Christmas Eve signals the end of the Advent fast. At the evening meal, *oplatki*, a small wafer reminiscent of the host and distributed by the priest, is broken and shared by the family. At midnight, Poles celebrate *pasterka*, the Mass of the Shepherds.

Another Christmas Eve custom is a visit from Star Man, a religious version of Santa Claus (and often played by the local priest in disguise). Star Man questions the children on their catechism. Those who know the answers receive presents; the less learned are scolded.

Because St. Francis of Assisi is credited with popularizing the creche, it is natural that in *Italy* the *presepio* (crib) is very important. Almost everyone displays one, including merchants and grocers. A custom that is rarely done now concerns the *pifferari*, Calabrian minstrels. For ten days before Christmas, they would go through the streets, playing their instruments at Marian shrines and carpenter's shops (in honor of St. Joseph). Italy is also the home of Befana. As legend has it, Befana was asked to accompany the Wise Men on their journey. She refused, but later changed her mind and went to look for them. She has never caught up with them, but on Epiphany visits homes and leaves candy in the stockings of good children—and a switch and a lump of coal to those who misbehave.

Midnight Mass is also a popular tradition in *France*, and following it families eat *le reveillon* (late supper). Before going to bed children leave their shoes by the fireplace for Père Noël to fill them with presents. Creches are a tradition in France, particularly in Provence where beautiful *santons* (small, handcrafted figures) are created throughout the year in preparation for the feast.

Across the channel in *England*, age-old customs of the type chronicled by Dickens and Irving continue to be observed. One old and painstaking custom occurs in Yorkshire with "Tolling the Devil's Nell." On Christmas Eve the bell of Dewsbury church is rung once for every year since the birth of Christ, the last stroke sounding at precisely midnight. This custom is believed to go back to the thirteenth century, when a local baron donated a bell to the church and had it rung each Christmas to remind him of his murdering one of his servants.

Germany, the home of the Christmas tree, begins its observation on the First Sunday of Advent. A wreath with four red candles is hung in a window on that day. The first candle is lit the Sunday after November 26, and a candle is lit for each of the two succeeding Sundays. The last candle is lit on *Heiligabend* (Christmas Eve). The Thursday before Christmas is *Klopfelnacht* (Knocking Night). Mummers in hideous masks go from house to house making all manner of noise. This ritual is said to ward off evil spirits and ensure fertility. German choir boys or *Kurrende* travel about singing carols. The favorite? "Silent Night."

HANUKKAH

Jewish people throughout the world celebrate Hanukkah (Festival of Lights) in December. Hanukkah lasts for eight days, and the actual dates change from year to year. This is because the Jewish calendar is lunar in basis rather than solar. The festival runs from 25 Kislev through 2 Tevet and usually falls sometime near Christmas.

The festival is rooted in both religious and seasonal events. Around 165 B.C.E., Judah the Maccabee led a revolt against the Hellenistic Syrians who ruled the Jews, and the revolt was successful. This fact alone seemed miraculous in nature. The temple was to be rededicated, and there was enough sacramental oil to burn for only a day. Miraculously, the oil burned for eight days, while more oil could be prepared. The festival is also believed to be tied in with the winter solstice.

In commemoration of this event, Jews light a menorah for the eight days of the festival. A menorah is a candle-holder with eight separate candles. One candle is lit for each day of the festival. This is the main custom connected with Hanukkah. A traditional and popular dish during the festival is potato pancakes. Many Jews also play dreidel, a game of chance derived from an old German gambling game.

Some Jews exchange gifts during Hanukkah. This gift giving is independent of the traditional exchange by Christians during the Christmas season. However, some Jews do not engage in the exchange of gifts in order to preserve the distinction between their festival and the Christmas season.

The major significance of Hanukkah for many Jews is the theme of religious freedom. Hanukkah commemorates a revolt that enabled the Jews to practice their religion free from oppression. Religious freedom is furthered when people know about and understand the customs and beliefs of others. At this time of year, it might be good for your family, particularly younger children, to learn about Hanukkah, which is celebrated so close to Christmas, yet is so distinct from it. If you have Jewish friends in the neighborhood, you might suggest that your two families get together to learn more about each other's traditions. The predominance of Christmas themes and the narrowness of a child's world can leave a child in ignorance of the fact that there is any other way of doing things besides one's own. This can be a time for children to learn about Jewish customs and in doing so, learn to respect differences. In this way, the theme of Hanukkah—religious freedom—and the theme of Christmas—peace on earth and good will to all—become more of a reality.

(See Bibliography for books of Hanukkah. If you are unable to get together with a Jewish family, you may wish to explore Hanukkah through reading and discussion.)

CAROLING

One of the great gifts of childhood is the youngster's ability to break into song totally unselfconsciously. Long before they learn to worry about pitch or whether they're hitting the right notes, small children will sing spontaneously—Top 40 hits, commercial jingles, songs they've learned at school or in church, tunes they make up themselves. Unfortunately, we lose this spontaneity as we grow up, and many of us can only break out in song in the privacy of the shower. We can learn a lesson from our children and begin again to appreciate the joy of singing, no matter what we sound like. And what better time to do this than at Christmas?

When we hear the word "carol" we immediately associate it with Christmas songs. This was not always so. Carols originally accompanied events other than Christmas, and were generally associated with revelry and an atmosphere of abandon. Needless to say, the Church of the early Middle Ages was not pleased with the custom.

St. Francis of Assisi (1181-1226) is generally credited with beginning the tradition of the popular sacred song. This paved the way for the redirection of the carol to holier themes. By the time of the Tudors, the carol is associated with Christmas, and beginning in the eighteenth century some of the

carols we are familiar with today came to be
written.

Church groups often sponsor caroling parties,
sometimes making up their itinerary by stopping at
the home of parishioners who are ill or
housebound. Groups also visit institutions and
sing for the residents. Family members might want
to get involved in activities such as these, or
perhaps get a group of their own together to go
out singing. Hot chocolate and cookies are an
enjoyable end to such an outing.

If going out to carol is not a possibility, make
caroling a part of your family activities at home.
Decorating the tree is a good time for singing.
Make an effort to learn some new songs,
particularly ones your children may have learned
in school. It doesn't matter that you don't sound
like Bing Crosby in *Holiday Inn*. Singing is twice
praying, as the saying goes, especially at
Christmas.

For some popular Christmas carols, see the Music
Book component of this program.

EGGNOG

Certain items appear on store shelves with greater
prominence and in greater quantity during the
Christmas season. One of these is eggnog, a
traditional holiday drink. You can buy your eggnog
at the store, or try this recipe and make your own.

Eggnog gets its name from the "noggin," a small

carved mug made of birch which was used to
serve drinks in English taverns.

6 eggs, separated
1 cup granulated sugar
1½ qts. thick cream
1¼ tumblers whiskey, brandy or rum

Beat egg yolks and sugar together until
lemon-colored, stir in well-beaten cream, stiffly
beaten egg whites, and liquor. Chill, place in
serving bowl, sprinkle cinnamon and nutmeg over
top.

(Taken from: *The Christmas Cook Book* by
Kathleen Epperson. San Francisco: Nitty Gritty
Productions, © 1969.)

GIFT-GIVING

From the secular point of view, the most
prominent aspect of Christmas is gifts. The
pre-Christmas season is devoted to buying gifts,
Christmas Day is devoted to giving them, and the
post-Christmas season exists for the sake of
exchanging them. As we celebrate Advent and
prepare for Christmas, how can we infuse new and
deeper meaning into the custom of exchanging
gifts?

The meaning of gifts: A gift is something freely
given. This sounds rather trite until we stop to
consider the number of gifts we give out of
obligation. Strictly speaking, these are not gifts at
all, but the result of social pressures or a sense of

obligation. To some extent, this type of "gift" will always be with us. However, there are some things we can do to make this type of giving more in keeping with the Christmas spirit. Sometimes people continue to exchange gifts out of habit, and both parties would rather put an end to the practice. Are there any people on your gift list whom you think might fall into this category? Some people will respond very positively to an honest discussion of the situation. In lieu of a gift, a call or visit during the Christmas season may come to mean much more.

A gift is really a part of ourselves. It's a sharing with another person and a way we show them that we care. As an alternative to the pressure to measure gifts in terms of cost, this might be a good time to consider other ways of giving to others.

Money vs. Value: Almost everyone's budget is limited. Children especially can feel the frustration of wanting to give a nice gift to a parent or other relative and not being able to afford to. What are some alternatives?

Making gifts: The biggest drawback to this is the time factor. The person who habitally shops during the last few days before Christmas is obviously in a poor position to give homemade gifts. With some advance planning, however, making gifts is fun, generally less expensive, and the product has a value that can't be measured in dollars and cents. Here are just a few of the possibilities:

• knitting, crocheting or sewing a garment
• ceramics

- a dried flower arrangement
- a macrame wall hanging or plant hanger
- a framed painting or photograph created by the giver
- a banner or collage
- a collection of favorite recipes, printed on index cards

All of the above presume a certain skill or talent on the part of the giver. Not everyone can paint, knit or have access to a kiln. Other creative gift ideas can be thought of and given in the form of "gift certificates," redeemable at a later date. For example . . .

- an evening of free babysitting for the parents of a young child or children
- a promise to clean the garage (basement, attic, "junk closet," etc.), when spring comes
- an offer to type for a family member in school who has a paper or report coming up
- a trip to a favorite place (museum, zoo, etc.), for a younger child who cannot travel unescorted
- lessons (you specify the number), about some skill you have that another family member would like to learn

The possibilities are only as limited as your imagination, and often involve no special skills on the part of the giver. One of the best things about such gift certificates is that they offer one of life's most precious gifts: time spent with someone you love.

"But he's already got three dozen ties . . .": When buying gifts, it's often difficult to think of something special, different and useful for a

person. There are only so many shirts, toys, and sweater sets that one person can use. How do we break out of the mold? Think of the interests and hobbies of those you're buying for. The avid theatre-goer or music lover might appreciate tickets to a play or concert. Someone with a particular interest could be given a book on the topic or a subscription to a magazine or journal related to his/her field. A family member with a hobby could use material related to it (new oils for the painter, some sheet music for the pianist, etc.). A gift that speaks so specifically to a person's interests or talents shows that you care, that you know what's important in that person's life and that you want to contribute to their growth as a person.

Even as we realize our limitations in buying for others, we are aware that for many people today the necessities of life are almost luxuries. At Christmastide, we look for ways in which our giving of ourselves can extend beyond our small circle of family and friends. Below are just a few ideas on how families can do this.

- Money. One of the first thoughts that comes to mind is a donation to a charitable organization or an extra gift to the parish. Members of the family could decide on where they would like their money to go, and then contribute according to their means.
- Clothing. Because many people receive new clothing at Christmas, they might want to go through closets and decide which of their used but usable clothing they would like to give away. An evening could be devoted to mending and

preparing old clothes for delivery to an institution that distributes such clothing.

- Gifts. The family can consult the parish or some outreach organization and "adopt" a family for Christmas. This might consist of being given pertinent information (age, sex, clothing size) of the family members, and then buying an article of clothing for each person in the family.
- Time. Christmas is a time of heightened awareness, both of joy and of loneliness. People who are in need of company throughout the year—nursing home patients, orphans, the chronically ill, the institutionalized—feel this loneliness more keenly at Christmas. Family members might like to get involved in visiting such persons, perhaps even committing themselves to regular visiting throughout the year. Institutions, such as foundling homes, are often in need of people who will do nothing more than hold and cuddle infants, giving them the individual attention that the professional staff does not always have time for, and which is so essential to the infant's well-being. Younger children in your family who cannot participate in such visiting can be part of the family's efforts by helping with such things as making cards, wrapping packages, etc.

Many of the suggestions here are general, and purposely so. They are meant to serve as starting points for your own discovery of what you want to do, are able to do, and what needs around you need to be met. Inquiries into programs run by your parish, diocese and civic organizations will also aid in discovering ways to bring some measure of Christmas joy and peace to others.

THE POST-CHRISTMAS SEASON (DECEMBER 26-JANUARY 6)

The ten days following Christmas are marked by two important feasts: New Year's Day and Epiphany. In the winding down after Christmas itself, these days can get lost in the shuffle, particularly the feast of Epiphany. A little advance planning can make these two days special celebrations for your family.

New Year's Day

The secular emphasis here is on New Year's Eve and the attendant partying. The Church's celebration of Mary on the Octave of Christmas (January 1) can lose its meaning if it is greeted by the exhaustion and hang-overs commonly associated with New Year's Eve. Family members might opt to attend a liturgy later in the day to assure that they are rested and alert.

New Year's is also known as resolution time. Sometimes we promise ourselves that we will make ten major changes in our lives, none of which can be sustained beyond the first few days of the new year. The family can get together one night before New Year's and discuss New Year's resolutions. Individuals might like to make a resolution, and the family as a whole can also decide on one thing they'd like to work on during the year. The point here is that it is better to make one resolution that we can reasonably stick to, rather than a number of promises that run the risk of being easily broken.

One point we frequently neglect is to express thanks for all we've received in the year gone by. As part of your New Year's celebration, each family member could bring to the dinner table a symbol of something that happened during the year for which that person wants to give thanks. Each person then shares the symbol he/she brought. Once again, keep in mind that younger children may need help in doing this, and should be aided (but not directed) by a parent or older child. The reading for New Year's day in all three cycles is Luke 2:16-21. After all symbols have been shared, someone can read this reading aloud and allow a few moments so that you, like Mary, can ponder what's been shared today in your hearts. A fitting close for this little service would be to share petitions for what we hope for in the new year—for ourselves, our family and friends, and the world.

Epiphany
This day marks the traditional close of the Christmas season. It's a fitting day for taking down your tree and other decorations, but if January 6 falls on a weekday, it might be more practical to "undecorate" on the weekend when more free time is available (at least in theory!). Even as all family members participated in putting the tree and other decorations up, it's important to share in taking them down. A parent who begins the new year with the task of dismantling the decorations alone is certainly getting the short end of the stick.

Make this admittedly tedious work more pleasant by organizing it, with particular people responsible for particular things, in accordance with their ages and abilities. This might be a good time to sing one last round of Christmas carols. A special treat planned for the whole family after the task is accomplished (sending out for pizza, homemade cookies, etc.), also helps to make the time pass more pleasantly.

If at all possible, leave the creche up until January 6, even if you take the tree down beforehand. At dinnertime, or when everyone is together during Epiphany Day, gather around the creche for a short ceremony commemorating the arrival of the Magi. The reading for this day in all three cycles is Matthew 2:1-12. This reading can be done by assigning parts to different people. One person is responsible for moving the figures of the Magi to the stable at the appropriate point in the reading. A young child whose lack of reading skills makes participation in the reading out of the question is an especially good candidate for moving the figures. The creche can be left up until the next day, and then packed away with the other Christmas decorations.

One final note: Christmas often finds us with a lot of things we don't want to save and will probably throw away. For example, you probably aren't going to keep the two hundred Christmas cards you so lovingly hung around the house. Sometimes foreign missionaries or people who work in institutional settings can make use of used Christmas cards. Investigate the possibilities of recycling some of your Christmas material.

BIBLIOGRAPHY

Advent Calendar
Abbey Press
St. Meinrad, Indiana 47577
Publish a catalogue that offers a variety of
Advent/Christmas material.

Sacred Design
840 Colorado Avenue South
Minneapolis, Minnesota 55416
Distributors of the kit for making the Advent
Cube.

Martin, Herbert. *Advent Chain of Stars* (book)
Augsburg Publishing House
426 Fifth Street
Minneapolis, Minnesota 55415

Mary
Behold Your Mother, Pastoral Letter of the U.S.
Bishops (1973).
Available with study guides from: United States
Catholic Conference, 1312 Massachusetts Avenue
N.W., Washington, D.C. 20005

Marialis Cultus, Apostolic Exhortation of Pope
Paul VI (1974).

O Antiphons
The Twelve Days of Christmas Kit, designed by
Grailville Writing Center and available from The
Liturgical Press, Collegeville, Minn. 56321

Hanukkah
The Jewish Catalog, compiled and edited by
Richard Siegel, Michael Strassfeld and Sharon
Strassfeld. Philadelphia: The Jewish Publication
Society of America, 1973.

Union Home Prayer Book, compiled by the
Central Conference of American Rabbis.
Philadelphia: Maurice Jacobs, Inc., 1951.
Contains a service for each night of Hanukkah.

Creche
Nold, Liselotte. *Cradling the Christ Child.*
Minneapolis: Augsburg Publishing House, 1965.

Perry, Margaret. *Christmas Card Magic.* Garden
City: Doubleday & Co., 1967.

Coskey, Evelyn. *Christmas Crafts for Everyone.*
Nashville: Abingdon Books, 1976.

Ethnic Customs
Foley, Daniel J. *Christmas the World Over.*
Pennsylvania: Chilton Book Co., 1963.

Henderson, Yorke, et. al., *Parents' Magazine's
Christmas Holiday Book.* New York: Parents'
Magazine Press, 1972.

FAMILY SHARING PROGRAM

TELL ME A STORY:
A Family's New Year Journey Into Who They Are, Where They've Come From and Where They Might Be Going

Kathleen Szaj

SOME PRINCIPLES FOR USING THIS PROGRAM:

1. There are many possibilities inherent in this program. It has been used successfully with adults, with adults and teenagers and in a family setting. Ideally, your new year's journey should take place in five sessions within a day-and-a-half to two-day time period. These five sessions could also be done one per week over the course of five weeks. However, depending on your family's needs, energy and time, completing the entire journey of five sessions may prove impossible. Because the program is flexible, you can choose some of the ten activities given here and concentrate on them.

2. Please read through the *entire program*. After you have done so, decide on the number of activities you are going to do. After you have read through the principles, read the section

below (A, B, C, or D) that corresponds to the number of activities you will be doing.

3. Wherever possible, center what you do around a meal. The meal takes place before the activity.

4. If you do more than one activity, do them in the order in which they are found in the program (e.g., an activity about the past should precede an activity about the present).

5. There are options *within* a particular activity. Your choice depends on the personalities of those who will participate. Some people work better with words; some options include writing. Other people prefer to deal with objects and symbolism; there are options geared to this kind of activity. You are the best judge of which option to use.

Now that you have read the entire program and decided on the number of activities you will do, read the section below that pertains to you.

A. If you are doing One Activity, choose *either* of the following:
a. Personal Story Line/Personal Journal. Precede this with a meal, if possible.

or

b. Evening of Celebration.

B. If you are doing Three Activities, choose *either* of the following plans:
a. Pick any three successive meals and do the stories related to them;

or

b. Pick one story related to the past, one story related to the present and one story related to the future. Remember to tell the story to yourself first and then share it with the group.

C. If you are doing Five Activities, choose *either* of the following plans, doing the five activities in the order listed:

a. Personal Story Line/Personal Journal, a story related to the past, a story related to the present, a story related to the future and the Final Story;

or

b. A story related to the past, a story related to the present, a story related to the future, the Evening of Celebration and the Final Story.

D. If you are doing All activities, simply follow the directions given throughout the text.

A PREFACE:

We are a storied people. These stories are our identities as well as our gifts. Jesus knew that; he saw himself as the Father's story of love for humankind, for all creation. He knew that being his Father's story meant that when he revealed himself (told his story), he simultaneously revealed the Father. The story Jesus told with his life is a love story of a relationship between a Father and his people. Jesus told that story by *being* that love story (incarnation). And so must we.

When we give/tell our stories to ourselves and each other, we are also becoming the Father's love story in the flesh. When we give/tell *our* stories, we also tell stories about God, about being "in love" with his presence in care-filled, wonder-full, life-affirming moments; and about "falling out of love" with ourselves and each other in bitter, frustrating, cruel moments of giving up on life. It is our legacy to be this falling-in falling-out story; it is also our inheritance to proclaim it. It is a sacred trust.

During the Advent-Christmas season, we become especially aware once again of the stories that help to identify us (as members of a family, as Christians, as North Americans, as part of all humankind) and often, family Christmas rituals reflect some kind of story-telling and story-listening. Families need, at this time of year, to again remind themselves from where they have come, who they are now and to where they might be going in the future. Old stories are told and re-told countless times year after year, and new ones are slowly created and welcomed, too. These stories become a way of bonding many individual family members' stories into ones that are greater still: that of families, neighborhoods, societies, creeds, nations and all other large "family" groups. In these stories, we tell each other that indeed, we *do* belong—to ourselves, to each other, to a Father who cares. In these stories, we gift each other with the Christmas present par excellence: the presence of ourselves, sometimes offered in a trembling question: "Will she/he accept me, listen to me, care about me?" It is a most holy gift.

It is the Advent-Christmas season now; one in which the stories of Jesus' beginnings and the perpetual wanting and waiting to renew our own beginnings interweave into some fragile hopes with which we decorate our Christmas lives. We hope to be healthy, to be together, to be happy, to love and be loved. We turn to the story of Jesus' coming to help us create this hope; to trust that just as Jesus is somehow born again every year, so too, our lives can be refreshed, renewed and re-blessed. Celebrating the stories of Jesus' birth assures us that this is true. We *can* make these coming days a *new year*.

These next pages are about that creation of a new year, about those stories we must proclaim as our birthright, about this Jesus and his Father whose stories are inseparably entwined in ours. These next days of following these pages (as they lead you into the telling of and listening to your stories) will see you journeying on roads that are at once profoundly human and religious. As you begin, you will be equipped with two special reminders to guide you along the way: "To be a person is to have a story to tell" and "You can't tell who you are unless someone is listening" (both travel aids supplied by author Sam Keen). With the promise of a special retreat/journey ahead, you are now ready to follow the map provided.

As you will notice, each session begins with the preparing and sharing of a meal which provides the initial setting for an exchange of fragments about the past, present and future. These most special events of human nourishment will also provide some needed relaxation, trust in others

and confidence in family members' own ability to
create and tell their stories. Shared mealtimes,
then, are crucial moments of refreshment in the
journey.

The next step along the way involves some adult
member(s) of the family helping to introduce the
focus for that particular session by centering in on
ways Jesus revealed himself to others, as witnessed
in John's Gospel especially. The adult leader is
encouraged to employ the passages in John (some
are listed in the instructions for each session) in
whatever creative manner she/he feels drawn to
explore. The younger family members, often
vividly imaginative, might be helpful consultants
here.

Some of the sessions will focus primarily on the
creation of one (out of two possible choices)
ongoing story project(s). During these times, *each*
family member will have the opportunity to work
on her/his own "personal story-line" *or* "personal
journal." (Both of these are described in fuller
detail later.) You may need to discuss with your
family their particular needs for privacy or sharing
for these two projects. It is strongly suggested that
each member be allowed to remain as private or
public as she/he wishes in showing other members
either their story-lines or personal journals. It may
be helpful to note that if some family individuals
have greater needs for privacy in their ongoing
story-telling project, they may wish to choose the
personal journal which can be kept as a strictly
private endeavor, instead of the more openly
revealing story-line. If such privacy is desired,

families may want to discuss together what it means to respect the private needs of others.

A similar kind of aloneness is needed by family members to take another step in the story-telling journey: after selecting a particular question or optional activity as a basis for a new story, each family person is to take her/his needed materials to some place in the story-telling room or elsewhere in the house where she/he can experience some space and silence. It is here that she/he will hold a private story-telling and listening session with *her/himself,* not as a rehearsal for the subsequent group sharing, but as a tremendously needed way to make friends with ourselves. We *need* us to tell us our own stories; and we need to listen with the same amount of care that we would give in listening to someone else dear to us. As this self-story-telling and -listening process is done, it becomes easier for one to value oneself and it becomes easier to tell these stories to others.

The following step is a natural next event in this story-telling and -listening process. Each person is given the sacred, attentive presence of the other family members, as she/he carefully unfolds her/his particular story revealing past, present and future dreams, anxieties, blessings, gifts and wounds. It cannot be overly stressed: the gift of active listening will be *the* present needed and wanted by family storytellers. It is yours to give and receive.

The three "ending celebrations" (one at the conclusion of the first evening; the second, encompassing the whole next evening; and the third, tying together the entire story-telling and -listening event) are important landmarks in the completion of one part of the journey (story) and the beginning of another. *Do* include them along the way; though an infinite number of interruptions are possible in family life—and this family retreat might not provide any exception—it is possible to continue the story journey, incorporating these inevitable interruptions along the way. The long supper-and-evening-afterward time period of the second evening could be such an opportunity; perhaps a family celebration of the present for that evening could be to attend a son or daughter's basketball practice or game, or school activity or whatever; or any other event that could be seen as an intrusion into the family retreat rather than an additional gift.

The final story—composed of the family's experiences in this journey undertaken together—is the gift of solidifying, clarifying and declaring as holy this time of revelation and acceptance. It is a story to end one journey and begin another as a renewed family who celebrate one another's transitions from past to present to future. It is an imperishable gift to treasure always. You are this living gift that increases in size and value. You Are That Story. Happy New Year!

Needed time for those who are completing the entire program: five sessions of three to five hours each (this includes mealtimes):

Session 1:
First day evening (supper and session): From Where Have We Come (the Past).

Session 2:
Second day morning (breakfast and session): Transition from Past to Who We Are Now (the Present)

Session 3:
Second day afternoon (lunch and session): More on Who We Are Now

Session 4:
Second day evening (supper and Evening of Celebration): Anticipating Where We Might Be Going (Future)

Session 5:
Third day morning (breakfast and session): the Future and So Forth

Needed Atmosphere
Any room that is conducive to story-telling with conditions like comfortable, close-together seating, warmth, color, room to spread out various materials used would be helpful. Added features such as carpeting or a large rug on which all family members might sit (a kind of "story-telling circle"), a usable fireplace and/or a plentiful supply of

candles, soft music, plant life, etc., can add special
touches in the creation of an intimate, trusting
climate among family members where the sacred
gift of story-telling and listening might be
exchanged.

Needed Materials
large supply of magazines and newspapers from
which pictures and words can be torn
large sheets of colored paper (any size you can
obtain can be used)
pencils, pens, marking pens of assorted colors,
crayons
Bible (preferably New American or Jerusalem)
For Optional Activity (*see second day afternoon
session*):
Choose one or two of the following objects;
gather enough of these so that each family
member might have one:

eggs
glasses of water
plants
lit candles
pieces of bread
bananas

For Optional Activity:
a new notebook for each member of the family (at
least 6″ × 8″) to be used for personal journals

SESSION 1—FIRST DAY: EVENING

From Where Have We Come –the Past
Family members can help each other to begin to

remember the memorable events and moments of their past and prepare each other to re-establish a trusting bond with one another by taking active part in the preparation and sharing of the supper meal. Just before or during the time the meal is being prepared, ask *each* family member to bring some tangible article for *each* of the *other* members that will remind these members of some event or moment in their pasts. Some possible suggestions: baby pictures or other photographs from the past, clothing articles worn in the past, any souvenirs acquired in past events, gifts received long ago, etc. Encourage family members to be as imaginative, thoughtful and humorous as possible in their selection of old momentos for other family members. Exchange their gifts of the past during the supper meal.

After the completion of all supper materials: Begin The Story Together (about 15 minutes)—in an atmosphere of warmth, low lights and soft music if desired. Family begins with sitting comfortably close to one another, as if ready to listen to a wonderful story. Parents or an adult family member can begin by letting their family members know how they came to decide to do their family retreat, why they have selected these story-telling and -listening sessions to share with their families and what does "having a story" mean. Do this beginning explanation in any way you choose to be most effective; you may decide that you wish to tell about the importance of story in some story form. Use the introductory remarks on gift-giving and story-telling as some suggested content if you find this helpful. In your explanation/story, try to respond to these two questions: Whose story am I

(are we)? and What story is mine (ours) to tell?
Other family members may want to help
contribute to this introduction; encourage this and
you will be affirming that all of us (from the
moment we are born) have a story inside us
deserving to be told and heard.

Now you are ready to travel into the past once
again. Asking the question from where did we
come, remind the family that this is a question that
humankind has been asking one another since the
beginning of human communication. It is also a
question the Jews asked of Jesus in his time; one
in which the Jews presumed to know the answer.
Jesus' reply is always: I come from the Father. (See
John 5:36-38; 5:19-23, 25-26; 6:44-46; as some of the
frequent times Jesus tells from where he has come
and therefore, who he is.) Just as we come from our
parents, so too, do we also come from countless
generations of ancestors and the Father as well.

Story-Telling and Listening: Alone—Each family
member may choose to tell a story using one of
the questions below *or* family members may
choose to do the optional floor plan activity
instead. Please advise family members that once
they have selected their activities for this session,
they are to use the next 20-30 minutes (depending
on family need) *alone*, carefully selecting a
question, creating a story to respond and finally
telling this story to one's self in private. This
private story-telling and -listening process is vital
prior to the group story-telling and -listening.

Activity: Story Statements (about 30 minutes)—After reading through the following, choose one that is important to your past. Then, looking through any available magazines, newspapers or other pictures around the house, find one picture that will help you to tell your story of the statement you chose. Then, tell yourself this story.

For Adults and Teenagers — choose one
1. When I was very young at the age of _____, I saw my parents as _____.
2. When I was a preteen/teenager, two things that scared me most _____.
3. I remember the day I discovered something very important about my sexuality _____.
4. One of the most joyful times of my childhood happened the day _____.
5. My favorite story about me growing up

_____.
6. The first time I met my future husband/wife I thought _____.

For Young People, Ages 8-12 — choose one
1. When I was about 5 years old, I thought my Dad was someone who _____ and my Mom someone who _____.
2. One of the most scarey times for me was when

_____.
3. One time that I realized I am a girl (boy) and not a boy (girl) happened the day that _____.
4. A really happy day for me was the time _____.
5. One story about me when I was very little that I like hearing is _____.

For Children Under 8

1. Something I remember about my Mom when I was very little _____.
   Something I remember about my Dad when I was very little _____.
2. One time when I was very little and scared this happened _____.
3. The way I found out I am a boy (girl) and not a girl (boy) _____.
4. A happy day for me was when

   _____.

OPTIONAL ACTIVITIES

For Adults and Teenagers
Draw a floor plan of the house you lived in when you were 8 years old. Include some of the following: your favorite room (color, location of furniture and objects), any rooms you were not allowed to enter, your bedroom (color, location of furniture and objects), places you went to hide when you were frightened or lonely, any rooms or corners you didn't like, etc.

For Young People, Ages 8-12
Draw a picture of your favorite room of the house you lived in when you were five. Draw in as much furniture and other objects (rugs, lamps, plants, books, pictures, etc.), as you can remember. Try to draw all of these in the colors that you remember them to be.

For Children under 8
Draw a picture of your first bedroom that you can remember. Draw in such things as the colors of

the walls, where your bed was placed, where your toys were kept, things hanging on the wall, where your clothes were placed, etc.

Story-Telling and Listening: Together (about 1½-2 hours)
Now take turns among family members telling and listening to the various stories of the past.
Remember to use the pictures you selected or the drawings you did to help you tell your story.
(Note: If your family is quite large you may want to break into several smaller units for the story-sharing, or remain as one unit for this process.)

END OF FIRST DAY: EVENING

At this time, family members can be told that each one will be working on a special, long-term story of their own, to be started and worked on during intermittent periods throughout the retreat. Once again, *each* family member may choose to do *one* of the following:

Personal Story Line
Family members look through any magazines and newspapers available, ripping out any words, symbols and pictures that are a part of their story (past, present and future). Family members who choose this activity should be told *not* to think too hard about the words, symbols and pictures they choose; they should allow their instincts to guide them in fairly rapid selection of these parts of their story. After tearing these out, each family member

will glue or tape these on to as many sheets of paper and in whatever fashion she/he chooses to help her/him tell her/his story. The stories can be shared later at appropriate moments. Also: other family members may help another who is doing his/her personal story-line by contributing any words, pictures, and symbols they find that seem to be a part of someone else's story.

Personal Journal
Family members who choose this ongoing activity will each receive a new notebook, which they will divide into three parts: the Past, the Present, the Future. From this point on, each member who keeps this journal has a personal record of the important memories, moments, feelings, thoughts, dreams and wishes of his/her life. Each "journalist" should be encouraged to write, draw, doodle, glue pictures of any other appropriate activity that will help him/her to tell his/her story. Each entry should be placed in the section most appropriate (Past, Present, or Future) and should also be *dated*.

Finally: To celebrate the end of this evening, choose and play a piece of music (with or without words) which helps to evoke and relive memories. After listening in silence, close with this or have family members contribute a last thought. (Some suggested music: "The Way We Were," Pachelbel's "Canon in D" or "Nadia's Theme.")

SESSION 2—SECOND DAY: MORNING (BREAKFAST AND SESSION)

Transition from Past to Who We Are Now (the Present)

While each family member contributes something toward the preparing and eating of breakfast, each must find something around the house that seems to best symbolize the person of the *next oldest* family member as seen through the eyes of the selector *at this present time.* Bring these symbols of the next oldest and share during breakfast. (Example: the person in my family born immediately before me is my older brother; to symbolize the person I see him to be at this time, I might bring a plant that has recently been separated from a larger parent plant and now has been placed in its own pot. I would then tell him that this new plant reminds me of him because he is just getting started on his own, establishing an independent home and family.)

After completing all breakfast materials: Each family member is to spend as much time as needed before lunch preparation to:

a. WORK ON STORY LINE—concentrating especially on finding words, symbols and pictures that help tell the story of the member's past and begin to talk about the evening (or see previous evening's instructions for details); or,

b. WORK IN PERSONAL JOURNAL—concentrating any entries of writing, drawing, picture-pasting, etc., most especially in the section of the journal labeled as "the Past" and beginning some entries for "the Present." Those choosing this might also wish to decorate the cover of this personal journal, create special dividers indicating "Past," "Present," and "Future" sections and add any other desired imaginative touches.

SESSION 3—SECOND DAY: AFTERNOON (LUNCH AND SESSION)

More on Who We Are Now

As each family member contributes some effort for the sharing of lunch, each must be thinking of some possible ideas of how best to celebrate who the family is now, separately as individuals as well as together. This celebration will begin with the remaining evening. Family members should exchange the various possibilities, but wait until after the following session to make a group decision.

BEGIN THE STORY TOGETHER (For an adult leader to communicate in any appropriate way): We are now ready to journey from the past and continue on into the present. The present tells us about who we are now, with the kinds of experiences, fears, doubts, joys and beliefs that make up how it is we see ourselves, others, and the universe that surrounds us. The present helps us to proclaim our identities.

Jesus also needed to identify the kind of person he was and this he did often through the use of stories, images, and symbols to reveal himself to others. Thus, when he told his listeners that he is "light," "true vine," "living water," "bread," "good shepherd," etc., they understood some special things about this man who lived among them. (See Jn 4:4-19; 6:35-40, 48-51; 7:12, 19, 27-28, 37-38; 10:7-18, 27-30; 11:25-26; 14:6-21; 15:1-8; 17:20-26; 18:37 for some of the many instances of Jesus' revelation of himself.) You may want to spend some time now or in the future sharing these ways Jesus spoke about himself and exchanging insights about what kind of man you can depict and know from such images. Is this someone you want to know from such descriptions of himself? If you were to choose a few images and symbols to describe how each of you knows himself/herself, what would these be? "I am a deep ocean," "I am a precision-tuned TV." (Try to use a combination of both ancient, natural symbols and those more recent technological-type symbols that are representative of our present age.)

Story Telling and Listening: Alone (about 30 minutes)—*Each* family member is to choose either (a) the creation of a story focusing on the present based on one of the story sentences below, once again selecting one picture from any available magazines, newspapers or other sources:

For Adults, Teens, Pre-teen 9-11
1. One thing I find myself worried about these days _____.
2. In my life, Jesus is someone who

   _____.
3. Something that is very precious to my life right now _____.
4. My relationship with my parents is one that ___.

5. One of the best things about me as I am today
   _____.

6. Something about me/my life that I would like to
   change _____.

For Children Under 8
1. One thing that worries, bothers or makes me
   unhappy at present is _____.
2. To me, Jesus is someone who
   _____.
3. Something very special in my life is
   _____.
4. My feelings about my Mom and me are _____.
   My feelings about my Dad and me are _____.
5. One very good thing about me is
   _____.
6. If I could change something about myself, I
   would _____.

or this option:

(b) the creation of a story using object symbols.
After selecting one or two of these symbols, each
storyteller is to "listen" inside himself/herself as
the selected objects help to tell who she/he is in
the present. The storyteller might begin by saying
to himself/herself: "This egg (banana, plant, etc.),
reminds me of who I am at present in these ways:
_____."

(Note: All family members electing to do this
option could use the same object symbols for the
whole family—you will then need to have enough
for all who wish to do this option—or you might
decide to locate some of each symbol mentioned
so that family members have a wider range of
choice.)

Object Symbols:
egg
glasses of water
plants
lit candles
pieces of bread
bananas

Story-Telling and Listening: Together (about 1½-2 hours)
With the aid of the pictures and object symbols, give each member an opportunity to share these stories of the present. Once again, encourage the creation of a complete story—other family members might help to draw out a shy storyteller—and full, attentive, genuine listening to these stories. It is very important that we feel that we are worth listening to. Only we can give that to one another.

(Note: If there is time before supper, individuals might work on "the Present" in either story lines or Personal Journals.)

SESSION 4—SECOND DAY (SUPPER AND SESSION): AN EVENING OF CELEBRATION

After the completion of the stories, family members should now decide with each other how best to celebrate your family as it is in the present, with all the uplifting as well as more negative experiences your family shares.

The following are only a few of the many creative endeavors you might choose for this evening's celebration; *do* feel free to add any of your own:

1. Go out to dinner as a family; afterward attend a play, concert or film together whose subject is the celebration and reverence of being alive, special and loving right now—today!
2. Prepare and share dinner at home together, cooking some of each family member's favorite food; afterward, attend a play, concert or film as described above.
3. After preparing and sharing the supper meal together at home, select a program on TV that will help all family members celebrate who they are as individuals and as belonging to your family *now!*
4. After sharing supper together, make a list of each family member's favorite things to do; spend the rest of the evening trying to do (as a family) *one* favorite thing of each member (the larger the family, the more simple that activity might have to be in order to do a favorite of each).

    or

    After making that same list of favorite activities, decide which one or two you will do this evening and then establish a "calendar of upcoming favorites" for the remaining activities; mark these plans as definite future events on the family calendar. (If the family doesn't have such, you might consider creating or purchasing a large 12-month calendar with ample space for writing in family activities; you might also consider this as an activity for the evening.)

5. After sharing dinner together, have each family member contribute a story (written or oral) that she/he wishes to hear read or told; family members can then take turns reading or telling each of these or the family could elect *the* storyteller for the evening.

6. After sharing dinner together, take a poll of all family members' favorite games; decide which to play this evening as a celebration of the present and which to save for other days. (If your family is unacquainted with game playing or undecided about which to play, some delightful help might be found in *The New Games Book* —Play Hard; Play Nobody Hurt by the New Games Foundation, edited by Andrew Fluegelman (Headlands Press Book, Dolphin Books/Doubleday & Co. Inc., Garden City: New York [1976]—paperback, $4.95).

7. After sharing dinner together, watch a favorite TV program as a family, especially paying close attention to the *commercials*! At the end of the evening, have each family member choose one commercial slogan that would best describe himself/herself as she/he is now and one slogan that would symbolize your family unit as it is now. (Example: A few years ago, a health spa ran an`ad on TV that I found particularly representative of my tumultuous life at the time: ''There's a new you dying to be born . . . you can start your life all over again . . .'')

8, 9, 10, etc. other possibilities you create.

ENDING THE EVENING:

Celebrate and conclude this evening by gathering together in the story-telling circle and doing one of the following:

1. Each family member takes a turn telling each of the other members a reason why she/he is glad to know/be with each of the other family members.
2. Each family member takes a turn telling each of the other members "good-night" in any way she/he wishes.
3. The family stands close together to form one big "family hug."

SESSION 5—THIRD DAY: MORNING (BREAKFAST AND SESSION):

The Future and So Forth
Begin this last session of focusing on the future and integrating the past, present and future into one story by preparing and sharing a breakfast meal together. Have each member come to the table wearing some item of clothing, jewelry or other accessory that expresses his/her hopes for the future. (This can mean individual personal future, family future, destiny of a certain group of people, destiny of the nation, world, universe, etc.) Take turns during the meal exchanging the meaning of these worn items.

After all breakfast rituals are completed, spend some needed time (about ½ hour) focusing on the future by working on the story-lines or adding entries into the personal journal.

Story-Telling and Listening: Alone
Each family member is to choose one of the
following statements as a basis for telling stories
about the future (again using the pictures available
as guides) or instead choose to do the optional
activity described below.

STORY STATEMENTS

For Adults, Teenagers, Pre-teen
1. As I see myself ten years from now, I'd like to _.
2. Something I worry most about in the future ____.
3. A skill/talent/gift that I would like to develop in
   myself in the next few years _____.
4. Some condition in the world that I plan to
   change _____.

For Children Under 8
1. When I am ten years older I think I will be ____.
2. When I think of me growing up, I feel worried
   about _____.
3. Something special I would like to learn how to
   be or do is _____.
4. Something wrong or unjust in the world that I
   will help change _____.

or

Find something that belongs to you that describes
the kind of person you want to become in the
future. Let this item help you to tell yourself this
story of who you want to be, and listen carefully to
your own story. Bring this item to the family group
later. (Example: I might bring a box of crayons,

chalk, paints, etc., to let my family know I want to be someone who adds life and color to those others who will be affected by me. I would then create a story about this future colorful me.)

Story-Telling and -Listening: Together
Each family member should have the opportunity to tell his/her stories of the future as before.

The Final Story
With bread and wine to be shared signs of nourishment of family members with/for each other and the presence of Jesus who lives among us especially when we nurture each other with such things as stories; and with each member's story lines and/or journals in hand, gather close together as a family, sitting in the story-telling circle. Re-create aloud the story of the past day and a half: of whom the family members have been with as well as for one another, of the kinds of stories told and heard, of the shared meals and other nurturing moments of the two days. One of the parents or older children might begin this final group story in a manner such as this:

Once upon a time not so long ago, there was a certain family whose names were *(perhaps different family members will fill in these blanks—ask them to help you tell the story).* Now, this family gathered together to _____ and so on the first evening when they came together they decided to _____. This (these) they did by _____. After listening, this family discovered their stories were about _____, and the family felt _____ to hear them.

Continue the story, making this last story as long as family members wish to create, encouraging contributions from all members. Reinforce the feeling of "Yes, I *belong* to that story—it is *mine* and *ours* to tell and listen." If there are fears or is hesitation about helping to create this family story spontaneously, an adult member's gentle leading could be the stimulus needed. Help each other to believe that you are all born storytellers and each family member is a rich store-house of creativity, imagination and story. Summarize and celebrate your story-telling and -listening experiences of these last hours spent together in this last story . . . and live happily into the new year.

"God made [people] because he loves stories."
Elie Wiesel

CHRISTMAS TRADITIONS IN SCRIPTURE

THE MEANING OF CHRISTMAS TRADITIONS

Rev. Lawrence Boadt, C.S.P.

How to use this section

Christmas Traditions in Scripture offers rich background for understanding and bringing to life some seasonal traditions in Scripture.

This section can be used for personal reflection and enrichment by reading one section at a time.

As a family there are numerous ways to utilize the material here. A parent, adult or older child could read about one symbol, e.g. the star, and prepare an informal explanation to tell to the family during supper.

Some families would enjoy making a replica of the symbol afterwards to be hung on the tree or used as a decoration for the home.

Introduction

The feast of Christmas is traditionally a wondrous time of year for all, a time when the child in us is freed to see afresh. We put aside our doubts, our smallness of heart, our built-up prejudices, even our cynicism, enough to be expansive, to give generously, and to enjoy things we normally set aside only for children. We capture for a short time the childlike spirit that Jesus called for in his disciples.

No part of the Gospel story is more wonder-filled than the narratives of Jesus' birth. Here an atmosphere of expectation and high hope has been created by the Gospel-writers, a series of wonderful signs that describe the coming of Christ, and prepare all of us, who have heard the stories told again and again, to recognize who this child really is.

Yet, to appreciate the Christmas story, it is most important to understand how different these first two chapters of both Matthew and Luke are from anything else in the Four Gospels. They are filled with the miraculous and the frankly unlikely, and contrast sharply with the sober accounts of Jesus' adult ministry. How much historical information they contain is hard to judge. Many of the events surrounding the birth of Jesus may be loosely based on particularly striking phenomena that people many years afterwards recalled happening back about that time. The visit of wise men or the appearance of a sudden star could be such an event. But surely the birth accounts are the latest parts of the Gospels to be put together; and even such vague remembrances that could be recalled after 70 years or so will be mixed, as are all traditions handed down orally for any time at all, with exaggerations and typical heroic details. It is a particularly difficult question to answer "What is the historical fact?" First of all, none of the characters mentioned ever appears again in Christ's life except his Mother and John the Baptist; and John dies just as Jesus begins his work. Second, although both Matthew and Luke tell of Christ's birth in Bethlehem, this is about the only point on which they agree. Each seems to be unaware of any of the material the other contains; and in some parts, such as the genealogies, they show embarrassing contradictions. We just cannot be sure if any of the details can be traced through the memory of Mary. Possibly, some do stem from her since Luke tells us that she "kept all these things in memory" (Lk 2:51).

But trying to specify the raw facts behind the present narrative is not the key to a rich and meditative understanding of the Good News that they contain. Both Matthew and Luke selected stories about Jesus' infancy that looked back past the individual pieces of information of his birth to the word of Holy Scripture that lies behind them. To the first generation of Christians among whom the Gospel took shape, the life of Christ revealed him as truly the Messiah and Son of God because it fulfilled the promises and the prophecies of the Old Testament. Thus each incident in the Infancy Gospel is written and told in the light of Old Testament hope. The principle so beloved of the Church Fathers is already at work here: "The New Testament lies hidden in the Old, and the Old Testament is made clear by the New" (St. Augustine). As we investigate the individual symbols and scenes of the Christmas story, it will become clear how much the telling is determined and enriched by the use of Old Testament quotations.

A second principle before the Evangelists is that the birth of Jesus was not unrelated to his ministry on earth, nor to his death and resurrection. On the contrary, what Jesus did in his later ministry is prefigured in his infancy. This is the last of three stages of development. The very first reaction of the disciples after Jesus' resurrection was to be totally absorbed in the *risen* Lord. With time, more concern was given to his ministry on earth—thus develops the Gospel of Mark. Finally, the Church realized that God's plan was already unfolding in the act of Incarnation itself, and so we have these added prologues of Matthew and Luke to underline that the birth of Jesus was indeed the first revelation of Christ to the world as God's Son, and it was to Jew and Gentile alike.

In considering the meaning of the symbols of Christmas that follow, we can deepen our appreciation of God's wise and merciful plan for salvation in sending his Son into our world by entering into the two-fold movement of the Infancy prologues. First of all, they sum up all that the past had hoped for, and second, anticipate all that Jesus would be in his ministry still to come.

THE HERALD ANGEL

The double appearance of the angel Gabriel in Luke, chapter one, to announce the joy of the birth of a new prophet, John the Baptist, and of a savior, Jesus, draws on a rich tradition of public heralds in the ancient world. It is hard for us to imagine a time with no newspapers, no radio and no television, a time when many did not read at all, a time when people depended on town criers for information. Important news was proclaimed by heralds sent out by kings and other high officials.

The Old Testament is filled with examples. The news was not always good. King David wept bitterly when the messenger brought word from the battle that his son Absalom had been killed (2 Sam 18). Some three hundred years later, in 701, another herald, this time from the great king of Assyria, demanded the surrender of Jerusalem or it would be destroyed. The king and his advisors were in despair until reassured by the prophet Isaiah (2 Kings 18 and 19). On the other hand, the news could be joyful, as when Solomon is proclaimed king in I Kings 1:34.

God, too, had his heralds. The Old Testament records the messengers/angels sent to Abraham to announce the birth of Isaac, or to Lot to rescue him from Sodom. Moses encounters an angel of the Lord in the burning bush announcing that God would set his people free, and an angel leads the people of Israel through the Red Sea and the desert (Ex 14:19, 23:20).

But God did not only make use of angels. He also had his prophets who understood themselves as God's messengers. Their oracles opened with the typical formula of the herald: "Thus says the Lord. . . ." More often than not, they had the saddening task of proclaiming judgment and punishment to Israel for her sins and rejection of God. But at other times, they could announce joyful hope, as when Isaiah promises a new David, Emmanuel, a God-hero, a father-forever, a prince of peace (Is 9:5). Or when Ezekiel proclaims that Yahweh himself will shepherd his people, leading them to new pasture, seek out the lost, heal the injured

(Ezek 34:15-16). Thus both angels and prophets bring God's will to men. Both are described as part of God's court in heaven, where they stand in his council and know his plans.

The angel Gabriel brings Good News to Zachary and to Mary. He brings news of the fulfillment of God's plan of salvation, fulfilling for the birth of the messiah the same role he played of interpreting for Daniel the Lord's care for his people in persecution in Daniel 9.

There is also the chorus of angels proclaiming to the shepherds the birth of Jesus in Bethlehem. They both herald a solemn event and reveal a glimpse of the heavenly court in praise of God's saving plan. Like the divine ambassadors of the Old Testament, they authenticate their news by pointing to the signs of its accomplishment: the manger, the swaddling clothes. These reveal what kind of king it is they announce.

We can, perhaps, appreciate more deeply the importance of the Christmas heralds by recalling for a moment the walls of the great Gothic cathedrals of Europe with their rows of prophets and kings of the Old Testament surrounding the statue of Christ. Each holds in his hand a banner with the words of an Old Testament prophecy about the Messiah on it. Thus they give silent testimony to the hope and patient waiting of the generations of Israel, and of the long line of kings of the house of David who lived'and died before the prophecy of a messiah was fulfilled. Another medieval custom that brings home the importance of the herald role of expectation was the Christmas play of the prophets in which the actors, dressed in the long white robes and beards of ancient seers, process into the church on Christmas Eve and one by one deliver a prediction from the prophet they represent.

Even today, the modern custom of sending Christmas cards can be a continuation of this prophetic and heralding role—if we are willing to make their message a personal one of faith and concern, and not just a commercial necessity. For Christmas is announcement of good news. The solemn proclamation of the angels forms a model of the Christian proclamation of the Gospel of Christ that spilled from the lips of Peter and Paul after the resurrection: a gospel of peace and joy, a proclamation of reconciliation, a conviction that God is indeed with us.

THE SHEPHERDS

Israel is a modern, bustling state, and the daily rumble of autos and jets fills the air of this time-worn land. In our urban world, we have forgotten many of the features of farm life that made Jesus' parables and images come alive to his listeners. Yet much still remains to remind us of quieter times long ago: a farmer sifting wheat with a pitchfork, a goatskin tent of a bedouin family by the side of a field, and above all, the shepherds tending their flocks of fat-tailed sheep.

This timeless picture of care and concern was popular in the ancient Near East. The kings of

Babylon in the eighteenth century before Christ
claimed with pride that the sun god Shamash had
made them shepherds of their people. The Old
Testament itself often uses the image of the
shepherd to describe a good king. Jeremiah and
Ezekiel both prophesy that God will raise up new
shepherds for Israel, like king David, who will not
care for themselves, but care for the people. The
prophets see these rulers as delegates of the true
Shepherd, God himself, who gathers his scattered
flock and brings them to new meadows to increase
and prosper (Jer 23:3-4). Beloved Psalm 23
expresses the ideal at its fullest: "The Lord is my
shepherd, I shall not want."

The flocks of sheep formed an important part of
the economic well-being of the villages and small
farms. They provided wool for clothes, milk and
cheese to eat, skins for parchment writing
materials, and meat for special occasions. A man
wealthy in flocks was considered wealthy indeed.
Sheep are quiet, unaggressive, affectionate,
defenseless, and easily able to wander off in
search of a tuft of grass on the barren Palestinian
hills. How important that the shepherd be able to
guide them and protect them, not only from wild
animals, but from their own unwitting
carelessness—many a lamb, reaching for one
more green morsel, has fallen over the edge of a
gully.

The life of the shepherd is not easy. The sheep
must be watched all day long. They must be
brought into a shelter at night and guarded. Each
morning, the shepherd goes to the gate of the

sheepfold and gives his special call, and his flock
immediately leave the others to follow him. If he is
sick or missing, how confused they are. Days of
rest are few and far between, days of protection
from cold and wind are rare. Despite the high
praises of leaders for the model shepherd, the
actual day to day life of the working shepherd
carried no honor and little reward. They formed
one of the lowest social classes in the ancient
world.

When the angels appear to the shepherds in the
fields to announce Christ's birth in Luke's Gospel,
it is precisely because they are despised and poor,
not because they are successful. Luke cherished
the announcement to these men, not much better
off than the sheep they tend, because he sees in
them a kindred spirit to the lowliness found in
Mary and Joseph, Elizabeth and Zachary. They are
the "anawim," the truly poor in life and in spirit,
who rely not on their wealth but on the hope of
God's promised savior. Luke passes over any
traditions he may have known about wise men and
important personages coming from afar, and
points instead to these humble shepherds as the
true witnesses to the miracle of Jesus' birth. Such
as these will later recognize the meaning of a
suffering savior, acknowledge a "king" who rides
into Jerusalem on a donkey, according to the
prophecy of Zechariah 9:9, in meekness and not
glory. It is to these poor that Jesus has come to
preach, as he makes clear to the delegates John
the Baptist sends to him to find out who he is:
"Tell John what you see . . . the poor have the
good news preached to them" (Lk 7:22).

Shepherds may not have the best world by human standards, but how well they fulfill the beautiful praises of Mary's Magnificat which proclaims that God "has looked upon his servant in her lowliness—all ages shall call me blessed!" Jesus understood himself in the language of high praise for the shepherd who really loved his flock. He is the Good Shepherd who knows his sheep and they know him; he finds the lost and gathers what the wolves scatter; he lays down his life for his sheep; he is moved with compassion for his people who are like sheep without a shepherd. In this same vein, the epistles of I Peter and Hebrews remind Church leaders that they too must be shepherds and pastors as Jesus was, the "great shepherd" (Heb 13:20) or "Prince of Shepherds" (I Pet 5:4).

This scene of proclamation to an unknown group of shepherds is more than another charming story told of Christmas. It immerses us in the Old Testament faith, waiting for God's ever-recurring saving acts. It signals us who read the account that Jesus' whole life is already taking shape before us: those to whom he will proclaim his kingdom, those who will receive his word, are present in anticipation. He, himself, is foreshadowed as the new shepherd promised of old, the new David, who was himself a shepherd from Bethlehem. He shall fulfill perfectly the prophecy of Micah 5:1-3 which foresees that from this smallest and most insignificant of towns shall come forth a new David to shepherd and rule the people of Israel by God's strength alone.

THE CHRISTMAS CRIB AND MANGER

The Christmas creche is perhaps the most popular of all religious customs at Christmas time, and yet one of the most recent. The ancient Basilica of St. Mary Major in Rome cherishes five sycamore boards said to be the crib in which Jesus was laid at his birth in the stable. These are first reported in the eleventh century, but are believed to have been there since at least the seventh century. Even earlier, in 440 A.D., Pope Sixtus had created a faithful replica of the crib of Bethlehem for the Basilica. But the first-known crib scene set up for popular devotion was the inspiration of St. Francis of Assisi in 1223, when he asked his brethren to prepare a representation of the nativity scene in the Italian town of Greccio just as St. Luke describes it in Bethlehem. Francis was so moved by the occasion that he, himself, read the Gospel and delivered the sermon at the Christmas Eve unveiling. The idea caught on quickly and a deep piety for the infant Jesus spread through Europe, especially in Germany and the Netherlands. Even Luther, the toppler of so many customs, maintained devotion to the nativity scene all his life, best expressed in the popular carol, "Away in a Manger," based on a stanza of one of his hymns. No church would be complete at Christmas season without its stable, figures of the Holy Family, wise men, and shepherds, along with the familiar ox and ass standing nearby.

Many customs have grown up around the crib, especially in European folk story that reflect the symbol of the crib scene as the praise of all creation, especially the animals and plants, for the

new king of the world, who was born so far from
the centers of human power and so close to
nature. In Eastern Europe mainly, there are tales of
how all the cattle bow on their knees on Christmas
night, and how the birds sing all night, and how
the bees awake from hibernation to hum a hymn
to Christ. The farm families often put straw under
the children's mattresses on Christmas Eve to
remind them that Jesus came in poverty many
years before. And following St. Francis' own
custom, they bring extra food to their farm
animals, especially the donkeys and oxen. In the
Middle East, a widespread story describes how all
the plants and trees bow toward Bethlehem on
that eve.

It is instructive to consider why such a rich
devotion was so late in catching on in Christian
thought. What did the earlier ages do? Even in the
Gospel, of course, Luke sketched the scene in a
few bold strokes only: "Mary wrapped the baby in
swaddling clothes and laid him in a manger
because there was no room for them in the inn."
No mention of the cave, of straw, of ox or ass. The
emphasis clearly falls on the fact that Jesus was
born an outcast from even the basic amenities we
would expect. But the picture suggests much more
than it tells. We know the typical stable of the
Bethlehem area was either the bottom floor of a
simple house with the family living above, or a
cave cut into the hillside beside the house. It was
primitive to say the least, and the smell and noise
can be imagined! Despite this spare portrait, when
the first known representations of the birth scene
appear on Christian sarcophagi in Rome about 343
A.D., we already see the ox and ass standing

beside the Holy Family. Imaginative, yes; but not entirely so. There was nothing particularly holy or sacred about either animal, yet they were chosen deliberately because the early Church naturally saw them as the symbols of how Christ's birth fulfilled all the great prophecies of the Old Testament. The very fact that Christ had been born in a stable called to mind the ringing prophecy that opens the Book of Isaiah:

> An ox knows its owner, an ass its master's manger,
> But Israel does not know, my people has not understood.

(Isaiah 1:3)

The early Christians understood all too well the meaning of this prophecy applied to Jesus' humble birth. Many of his own people could not accept a messiah who came as he did. In contrast, even the lowliest of work animals recognized *their* rightful stall. Thus the portrayal of the ox and ass at the crib stood for all who did understand the coming of Christ. It was not considered sentimental piety, but a lesson to be learned from the great prophet himself. The presence of these beasts in Christian art brings back the stinging reminder of Isaiah: God was received by the lowliest animals when he is overlooked by mankind.

The high Middle Ages took this idea of learning from the scene of Jesus' nativity even further. They replaced the manger and straw altogether with an altar on which the infant Jesus lay. To each side, Mary turns aside her glance or worships, and Joseph kneels to the newborn child. The medieval love of symbolism reveals itself in this scene. The manger has become the altar of the church, and the baby the prefigurement of the Eucharist as the sign of God's continuing presence to the world. The bread and wine conceal the sacrifice of the cross and resurrection, just as the humble birth concealed the true nature of Jesus and his ministry and revelation to come.

Whether through such symbols of faith or through the vivid creche of St. Francis, the humble birth in the stable has spoken to each age as a way of realizing how far indeed God came in sending his Son into our world—where he is received not by the powerful, but by the humble.

THE MAGI

The Greek historian Herodotus in the 5th century B.C. describes a Persian priestly class called *Magi* who specialized in dream interpretation, fortune telling, astrology, and divination. We know from such later Roman writers as Strabo and Plutarch that many still practiced their arts in Jesus' time. Some were known to be frauds, but even the great Cicero praised the best of them for their scientific methods and expertise in astronomy. The Bible, however, generally takes a very negative view toward all such diviners and astrologers with their secret lore. The religion of the Old Testament sees their attempts to know the future as a demonic effort to control God's will and lead the people into idolatry. In the New Testament, only Matthew's story of the wise men shows them in a favorable light. Need we recall the adverse character study of Simon the Magician who tried to buy the apostle's power in the Book of Acts?

Why then did Matthew alone see them positively? As with the previous symbols of the Christmas story, we are forced to look to the Old Testament prophecies, which played such a central role for Matthew in explaining the real meaning of Christ's life. The Gospel-writer undoubtedly knew the great vision of Isaiah 60:6 of a new day for Israel when:

Caravans of camels shall fill you,
Dromedaries from Midian and Ephah

and the glorious promise found in Psalm 72:10:

The kings of Tarshish and the isles shall offer gifts,
The kings of Arabia and Seba shall bring tribute.

Reflecting on such hopes, Matthew uses the story of the wise men to represent these gentiles coming from the far ends of the earth to acknowledge Jesus, the new king. Perhaps, too, he thinks of the messiah prophecy of Isaiah 11:10, which proclaims:

On that day, the Gentiles shall seek out
The root of Jesse, set up as a signal to the Gentiles.

Such biblical reflections have played a large role in later descriptions of the Magi as well. At first, the number of wise men in the tradition varied from two to twelve, but it soon settled universally at three, no doubt to correspond to the three gifts that Matthew mentions. Later tradition identified them no longer as mere astrologers, but as kings in fulfillment of Psalm 72. And they gradually came to be identified as rulers from the three major races mentioned in Genesis 9 and 10, the three sons of Noah: Shem, Ham and Japheth. By long tradition these had stood for the Semites, the Africans, and the Indo-Germanic peoples. Thus by the Middle Ages, one was always portrayed as black. In fact, to take the meaning one step further, medieval thinkers made one stand for old age, one for middle age and one for youth. So they were truly universal, representing all countries and all ages. As early as the fifth century A.D. we find them given names. In the beautiful mosaics of the Church of San Apollinare Nuovo in Ravenna, the three Magi, still dressed as Persian priests in baggy pants and pointed caps, are labeled Melchior, Balthasar, and Gaspar. It is Melchior, tall and elderly who bears the gift of gold; Balthasar, black and of sturdy middle age, who offers frankincense, while Gaspar, still beardless, brings myrrh.

Occasionally, other texts also played a role in enriching the meaning of these three familiar figures. That truly one should be black was proven by citing Psalm 68:32,

Let nobles come from Egypt,

And let Ethiopia extend its hands to God.

Even some distortions crept in! Medieval churches often show a scene of the wise men fleeing their burning ships. It seems later generations misunderstood "ships of Tarshish" to refer to Paul's home city of Tarsus. Thus the legend grew of Herod, who realized he had been fooled when he heard that the Magi were returning home by way of the sea to Tarsus, so he had all the ships in the harbor burned to prevent their escape. We know today that "tarshish ships" were the large ocean-going vessels of the Phoenicians long before Herod was born.

These devout little stories have taken us far beyond the simple biblical reflection of Matthew or Isaiah 60 and Psalm 72. But they accent the importance that all generations before us have given to how Jesus' life fulfills the Old Testament hopes. Matthew did not tell this story for amusement. He carefully places a scene of recognition by all nations at the head of Jesus' life as a prefigurement to the very last scene in the Gospel, when Jesus, at his ascension, commands his disciples to go forth to baptize all nations.

Matthew also does more. These men of good will have been led by nature to discover the new Messiah, but it can only take them so far. As the star disappears, they are forced to consult the Old Testament in order to complete their journey to its goal. In this sense, the magi bring the knowledge of the gentiles and submit it to the revelation of Scripture. At the same time, where wise men before had tried to thwart and destroy Moses and the patriarch Joseph before pharoah, or Daniel before the king of Babylon, these good wise men use their gifts to point out a new king greater than pharaoh, or Nebuchadnezzar of Babylon—or even Herod! He is a truly universal king for all peoples and all centuries.

THE GIFTS OF THE MAGI

The popular hymn "We three Kings of Orient are; bearing gifts we travel far . . . " reminds us of the importance in the ancient world of never visiting someone with hands empty. Every visit needed a special present chosen for the honored host. Thus the Queen of Sheba came from the farthest corner of Arabia to listen to the wisdom of Solomon, carrying many costly gifts befitting a king: gold, precious stones and spices (I Kings 10). Solomon in turn gave her all the wisdom she sought and valuable gifts besides.

Matthew wished to include the tradition of how wise men had come from the East to visit the new king, Jesus; and so naturally he describes them bringing gifts for a king, gifts worthy of Solomon himself. The same Old Testament reflection that led the Gospel writer to preserve the tale of wise men from the East as representatives of the gentiles, led him to draw the details of their gifts partly from the ancient prophecy of Isaiah about the glorious new day ahead for Israel when

>Caravans of camels shall fill you,
>Dromedaries from Midian and Ephah,
>all from Sheba shall come
>bearing gold and frankincense,
>And proclaiming the praises of the Lord.
>(Isaiah 60:6)

and partly from Psalm 45, where King Solomon is described fragrant with myrrh and his queen dressed in the gold of Ophir on their wedding day. Even Psalm 72, cited in the previous section on the Magi, promises that kings from Arabia shall bring gifts to Israel.

Nothing in their world was more mysterious to ancient man than the exotic land of Arabia. There, and there alone, grew the valued myrrh and frankincense trees with their sweet sap, which was collected in gum balls, just like the rubber from the trees of South America. These prized spices were shipped by camel and ship all over the known world to be burned in temples as a sweet smell before the gods. And myrrh was further used to help prepare bodies for burial and to counteract the terrible smell of death—even the Egyptians used it in mummification.

From reflection on these characteristics, one can easily understand that beautiful interpretation of the early Church, including possibly even of Matthew himself, that the gift of gold signified Christ's human kingship over the world; the temple frankincense, his divine nature; and the myrrh, his suffering and death to come.

Three gifts that tell more than meets the eye. All three not only mark how Jesus fills the prophecies of Isaiah and the psalmists for a new and glorious age, but themselves become prophecies of the future of this child, a future that hardly looks important in the poor, dark night of his birth. And it prepares us for more. Jesus is the great gift-giver, who returned the gifts he had received from mankind back to us more fully than we could ever imagine. In giving his life for us, he gave us life that needs no golden wealth, no sweet odor, and no embalming to keep it going.

Western tradition has kept alive the tradition of the Magi's gifts in the customs of gift-giving on Christmas or Epiphany itself, the feast of the three wise men. Thus, for example, in Italy, Lady Befana, a good fairy, brings her treasures to children on January 6. Other European nations celebrate with the story of how the child Jesus himself brings gifts Christmas night, or how St. Nicholas, on

December 6, sends gifts secretly at night to those most in need. In comparison, how washed out is our domestic tale of a Santa Claus with his arctic home and reindeer. For the religious legends tell not only a charming story, but have a lesson to be recited every Christmas. For, while rejoicing at the birth of Jesus, we are reminded of the gifts he brought first to us. And more deeply yet, we are prepared to give to others with as much generosity. Even in the celebration of birth, we should keep before us the parable of the Last Judgment, when the just shall ask of the Lord, "When did we see you hungry and feed you, or see you thirsty and give you drink?" And the king shall answer them: "I assure you, as often as you did it for one of my least brothers, you did it for me" (Mt. 25:37-40).

THE STAR

The journey of the wise men from the far ends of the earth to find their Savior summarizes the journey of us all through faith in this life. They are given light and direction by a star. Faith must in turn be a light of understanding for today. The star as symbol of heavenly light gives us a richer clue to the biblical story than do the scientific attempts at explaining such a marvelous star's existence.

Modern scholars have tried many times to find evidence of unusual heavenly occurrences around the time of Christ's birth. Some see the appearance of Haley's comet in 12 B.C. as the star of the Magi, though critics rightly object that no comet would appear to stand still over one house.

Others suggest a supernova, one of those sudden, bright, new heavenly objects that occur when an old star collapses into itself and explodes in some distant galaxy. Still others propose the conjunction of the three major planets, Jupiter, Saturn and Mars, in one heavenly zone, an event occurring about once a millenium. It happened in 7 B.C., and is an attractive proposal since such phenomena were often associated with changes of rulers in the ancient Near East.

In fact, trust in the message of such heavenly events was characteristic of the entire ancient world. Stories about the birth of Alexander the Great are connected with the appearance of a great star. Virgil describes the emergence of a new star at the birth of Aeneas, the founder of Rome, and it was widely reported that a special star was seen at the time of the first Roman emperor Augustus' birth. It is impossible for us to know whether the wise men of Persia or Judea noted such a sign at the approximate time of Jesus' birth. More likely, many years later after the disciples understood who Christ was, they associated dimly remembered heavenly spectacles of years ago with the birth of their Lord, who, after all, was so much greater than an Alexander or Augustus. And even more likely than that, their faithful reading of the Old Testament as prophecy led them to expect a star at the birth of the messiah and to understand its significance. Stars in the Bible are closely associated with the majesty of God and his manifestation.

On one level, they represent the beauty and joy of God's creation for the world. They are part of the

first creative act of God in the first chapter of
Genesis. Psalm 148 gives the command "All you
shining stars, praise the Lord," an idea even more
beautifully expressed in Job 38:7 which tells us
that the stars sang in chorus on the day of
creation.

But they are also more. The early poets of Israel
often picture the stars as "the sons of God" who
fight as his warriors against the enemies of Israel
(Judg 5:20). God, himself, is most solemnly titled
Yahweh Sebaoth, "Yahweh of the Hosts of
Heaven." Thus the stars are the special honor
guard of God's throne, and form the highest
reaches of heaven, above which God is seated in
majesty (Is 14:13-14).

The symbol of light which the stars represent also
plays a role in Israel's hopes for a new age of
divine salvation. Isaiah 60:1 cries out to an Israel,
despondent from the exile, "Rise up in splendor,
your light has come; the glory of the Lord shines
upon you!" And even the angels who announce
the Good News of Christ's birth to the shepherds
are bathed in the light of God's glory.

But most impressive of all is the expectation that
developed from the prophecy of Balaam in the
Book of Numbers that a star should herald the
Davidic messiah. The seer predicts "a star shall rise
out of Jacob, and a sceptre shall come forth from
Israel" (Num 24:7). Matthew points to the story of
the star because it signals the fulfillment of Old
Testament hope in the child Jesus, not because the
miracle occurrence seems so unusual to the eye.

Many instructive legends grew up around the star. St. Gregory of Tours in the fifth century tells the delightful custom of pilgrims to Bethlehem in his day, who would go to a certain covered well and put their heads under the darkened top to look into the water. If they were pure of heart, they would see the star of Bethlehem travel across the surface of the water. The medieval *Golden Legend* portrays the star in the hands of an angel, or with the face of an angel, to illustrate the divine guidance.

And the story of the star is not without modern lessons as well. How many people today rely on their horoscopes and believe in the quasi-scientific jargon of astrologers that they will learn their fates? All, we commonly say, have their stars. This type of faith is a far cry from the message of the star of Christmas which has no inner meaning in itself, but points ahead to the place where the true light dwells. It is not out of place here to sum up the value of the star as a symbol of Christ the Messiah by recalling the very reason why Christmas was established on the 25th of December. We, of course, have no idea from the New Testament on which day Jesus was born. But it seemed fitting to the Church to set the celebration at the time of the pagan festival of the Roman sun god to replace this pagan light with the true Sun of Justice and true Light of the world, Christ the Lord.

DREAMS AND GOD'S ANNOUNCEMENT

In the ancient world, dreams were an important

means of receiving word from the gods. In the Babylonian epic, the great hero Gilgamesh is given a vision of his friend Enkidu in the Underworld. Enkidu explains to the noble Gilgamesh the mortality of humankind. An Ugaritic myth from about 1200 B.C. tells how Daniel learned of the death of his son in a dream. Aeneas in Virgil's epic *Aeneid* receives the command to leave Carthage and go to Italy and found a new city, Rome. Every royal court had professional dream interpreters to help the king. Compare the great number at the court of King Nebuchadnezzar of Babylon in the Book of Daniel.

In general, the priests and prophets of the Old Testament accepted the idea that God occasionally chose to communicate to Israel through dreams. The Book of Numbers tells how God speaks to Moses face to face, while to the prophets he will speak in dreams and visions (Num 12:6). The young man Elihu tells Job in his despair that God regularly reveals himself through dreams in our sleep. And the Bible passes on the dream stories of how Jacob saw the ladder to heaven at Bethel (Gen 28), how God called to Samuel in the temple at night (I Sam 3), and how Solomon received his wisdom in the dream he had at Gibeon (I Kings 3). On the other hand, dreams were open to misuse, and the prophets are naturally wary of those who claim God's word from a dream. Jeremiah warns against their messages, calling them "lying prophets." Deuteronomy condemns prophets who preach a new religion because gods revealed themselves in a dream.

But there are two important dream stories in the

Old Testament that help us grasp the meaning of
the dream of Joseph and of the Magi in the
Christmas story. In chapter two of Daniel, alone of
all the wise men in Babylon, Daniel can interpret
Nebuchadnezzar's dream of the statue made up of
gold, silver, bronze and iron. The second incident
is in Genesis, where Joseph had to be called from
prison when pharaoh's astrologers and sages failed
to interpret the dream of the seven fat cows and
seven lean cows. In both cases, the hero receives
from God the meaning of the dream. Both stories
emphasize the point that knowledge of the future
from dream analysis is not in the hands of
magicians and professional interpreters, but comes
from God only when he chooses to give it.

This can be seen most clearly in two important
New Testament examples. In Acts 9:10, Ananias
has a dream ordering him to baptize Paul despite
his anti-Christian past. And in Acts 16:9, Paul
himself sees a man from Greece calling him to
come to Europe to preach the Gospel. Both
represent important moments when God uses the
dream to further his plan of salvation.

In Matthew, the dreams of St. Joseph, both at the
announcement of Jesus' conception, and at the
time of Herod's threatened slaughter, come
directly from God to ensure the safety and
direction of the new messiah's life. The same
holds true for the third infancy dream, that of the
Magi, which orders them to go home a different
way. The dream, like the herald's proclamation,
calls attention to an important event about to
happen. These dreams of Jesus' childhood echo

on two levels the later mission of Jesus. First, they prepare for a new era of the Spirit. St. Peter, in Acts, chapter two, preaches the first missionary sermon after the resurrection by citing the prophet Joel who foresaw a new age, when "your old men shall dream dreams, your young men shall see visions," and God will pour out his Spirit in those days (Joel 3:1). That is, God will once again communicate freely with humanity as of old because of the work of Jesus in sending the Spirit.

The second aspect involves the prophetic fulfillment of the Old Testament in St. Joseph's dream. A Jewish popular legend outside the Bible recorded that the birth of Moses had been announced by a dream to pharaoh, and like Herod, he had trembled in fear and ordered the slaughter of the Hebrew boys at the advice of his wise men. Thus Matthew relates the material about Christ's birth, gathered from a variety of sources, to the person of Moses, to prepare us to recognize Jesus as a new Moses, giver of a new law and a new Covenant in his ministry.

ADVENT/CHRISTMAS
SONGS

Adeste, Fideles

1. Adeste, fideles, laeti triumphantes,
   Venite, venite in Bethlehem;
   Natum videte, Regem angelorum.

   Refrain
   Venite, adoremus, venite, adoremus;
   Venite, adoremus Dominum.

2. Deum de Deo, Lumen de lumine,
   Gestant puellae viscera;
   Deum Verum, genitum, non factum.

   Refrain

Angels, from the Realms of Glory

1. Angels, from the realms of glory,
   Wing your flight o'er all the earth;
   You who sang creation's story
   Now proclaim Messiah's birth.

   Refrain
   Come and worship, come and worship,
   Worship Christ, the newborn King.

2. Shepherds, in the fields abiding,
   Watching o'er your flocks by night;
   God with man is now residing,
   Yonder shines the infant's light.

   Refrain

3. Sages, leave your contemplations,
   Brighter visions beam afar;
   Seek the great Desire of nations,
   You have seen his natal star.

   Refrain

                              James Montgomery

Angels We Have Heard on High

1. Angels we have heard on high
   Sweetly singing o'er the plains,
   And the mountains in reply
   Echo back their joyous strains.

Refrain
Gloria in excelsis Deo,
Gloria in excelsis Deo.

2. Shepherds, why this jubilee?
   Why your joyous strains prolong?
   Say, what may the tidings be
   Which inspire your heavenly song?

   Refrain

3. Come to Bethlehem and see
   Him whose birth the angels sing:
   Come adore on bended knee,
   Christ, the Lord, the newborn King.
   Refrain

                                    French Carol

The First Noel

1. The first Noel the angels did say,
   Was to certain poor shepherds in fields as they
        lay,
   In fields where they lay, keeping their sheep,
   On a cold winter's night that was so deep.

   Refrain
   Noel, Noel, Noel, Noel,
   Born is the King of Israel.

2. They looked up and saw a star
   Shining in the east beyond them far,
   And to the earth it gave great light,
   And so it continued both day and night.

   Refrain

3. And by the light of that same star
   Three Wise Men came from country far,
   To seek for a King was their intent,
   And to follow the star wherever it went.

   Refrain

4. This star drew nigh to the northwest,
   O'er Bethlehem it took its rest,
   And there it did both stop and stay
   Right over the place where Jesus lay.

   Refrain

5. Then entered in those Wise Men three,
   Full reverently upon their knee,
   And offered there, in his presence,
   Their gold and myrrh and frankincense.

   Refrain

   English Carol

God Rest You Merry, Gentlemen

1. God rest you merry, gentlemen, let nothing you
        dismay,
   Remember Christ our Savior was born on
        Christmas Day;
   To save us all from Satan's power when we
        were gone astray.

   Refrain
   O tidings of comfort and joy, comfort and joy;
   O tidings of comfort and joy.

2. From God our heavenly Father a blessed angel
     came;
   And unto certain shepherds brought tidings of
     the same;
   How that in Bethlehem was born the song of
     God by name.

   Refrain

3. "Fear not, then," said the angel, "Let nothing
     you affright,
   This day is born a Savior of a pure virgin bright,
   To free all those who trust in him from Satan's
     power and might."

   Refrain

4. Now to the Lord sing praises, all you within this
     place,
   And with true love and brotherhood each other
     now embrace;
   This holy tide of Christmas all others doth
     deface.

   Refrain

                                        English Carol

Hark! the Herald Angels Sing

1. Hark! the herald angels sing, "Glory to the
     newborn King;
   Peace on earth, and mercy mild, God and
     sinners reconciled!"
   Joyful, all ye nations, rise, join the triumph of
     the skies;

With th'angelic host proclaim, "Christ is born in
  Bethlehem!"
Hark! the herald angels sing, "Glory to the
  newborn King!"

2. Christ, by highest heaven adored; Christ, the
  Everlasting Lord!
  Late in time, behold him come, offspring of the
  virgin's womb;
  Veiled in flesh the Godhead see; hail
  th'incarnate Deity,
  Pleased as man with man to dwell, Jesus, our
  Emmanuel.
  Hark! the herald angels sing, "Glory to the
  newborn King!"

3. Hail, the heaven-born Prince of Peace! Hail, the
  Sun of Righteousness!
  Light and life to all he brings, risen with healing
  in his wings.
  Mild he lays his glory by, born that man no
  more may die,
  Born to raise the sons of earth, born to give
  them second birth.
  Hark! the herald angels sing, "Glory to the
  newborn King!"

Charles Wesley

It Came upon the Midnight Clear

1. It came upon the midnight clear, that glorious
  song of old,
  From angels being near the earth to touch their
  harps of gold:

"Peace on the earth, good will to men, from
heaven's all-gracious King!"
The world in solemn stillness lay, to hear the
angels sing.

2. Still through the cloven skies they come, with
peaceful wings unfurled,
And still their heavenly music floats o'er all the
weary world;
Above its sad and lowly plains they bend on
hovering wing,
And ever o'er its Babel sounds the blessed
angels sing.

3. O ye, beneath life's crushing load, whose forms
are bending low,
Who toil along the climbing way with painful
steps and slow,
Look now! for glad and golden hours come
swiftly on the wing:
O rest beside the weary road and hear the
angels sing.

4. For lo! the days are hastening on, by prophet
bards foretold,
When with the ever-encircling years comes
'round the age of gold,
When peace shall over all the earth its ancient
splendors fling
And the whole world give back the song which
now the angels sing.

Edmund H. Sears

Joy to the World

1. Joy to the world! The Lord is come:
   Let earth receive her King;
   Let every heart prepare him room,
   And heaven and nature sing,
   And heaven and nature sing,
   And heaven, and heaven, and nature sing.

2. Joy to the world! The Savior reigns:
   Let men their songs employ;
   While fields and floods, rocks, hills and plains
   Repeat the sounding joy,
   Repeat the sounding joy,
   Repeat, repeat the sounding joy.

3. He rules the world with truth and grace,
   And makes the nations prove
   The glories of his righteousness,
   And wonders of his love,
   And wonders of his love,
   And wonders, wonders of his love.

Isaac Watts

Lo, How A Rose E'er Blooming

(Tr. Vv. 1,2, Theodore Baker, 1851-1934
Tr. V. 3, Harriet R. Krauth, 1845-1925)

1. Lo, how a Rose e'er blooming
   From tender stem hath sprung!
   Of Jesse's lineage coming
   As men of old have sung.

It came, a floweret bright,
Amid the cold of winter,
When half spent was the night.

2. Isaiah 'twas foretold it,
The Rose I have in mind,
With Mary we behold it,
The Virgin Mother kind.
To show God's love aright,
She bore to men a Savior,
When half spent was the night.

3. This Flower, whose fragrance tender
With sweetness fills the air,
Dispels with glorious splendor
The darkness everywhere.
True Man, yet very God,
From sin and death he saves us
And lightens every load.

O Come, All Ye Faithful

1. O come, all ye faithful,
Joyful and triumphant,
O come ye, O come ye to Bethlehem;
Come and behold him,
Born the King of angels.

Refrain
O come, let us adore him,
O come, let us adore him,
O come let us adore him,
Christ the Lord.

2. Sing, choirs of angels,
   Sing in exultation,
   Sing, all ye citizens of heaven above;
   Glory to God
   In the highest.

   Refrain

3. Yes, Lord, we greet thee,
   Born this happy morning,
   Jesus, to thee be glory given;
   Word of the Father,
   Now in flesh appearing.

   Refrain

                                        John F. Wade

O Come, O Come, Emmanuel *(Latin Hymn)*

1. O come, O come, Emmanuel
   And ransom captive Israel,
   That mourns in lonely exile here
   Until the Son of God appear.

   Refrain:
   Rejoice! Rejoice! Emmanuel
   Shall come to you, O Israel!

2. O come now, wisdom from on high,
   Who orders all things mightily;
   To us the path of knowledge show
   And teach us in your way to go.

   Refrain

3. O come, O come, our Lord of might,
   Who to your tribes on Sinai's height
   In ancient times did give the law
   In cloud and majesty and awe.

   Refrain

4. O come now, Rod of Jesse's stem,
   From every foe deliver them
   That trust your mighty power to save,
   And give them victory o'er the grave.

   Refrain

5. O come now, Key of David, come,
   And open wide our heavenly home;
   Make safe the way that sets us free,
   And close the path to misery.

   Refrain

6. O come now, Dayspring from on high,
   And cheer us by your drawing nigh;
   Disperse the clouds of lowering night,
   And death's dark shadow put to flight.

   Refrain

7. O come, Desire of nations, bind
   In one the hearts of all mankind;
   Bid all our sad divisions cease,
   And be yourself our King of peace.

   Refrain

O Come, Little Children
(Christoph Von Schmid, 1768-1854, Tr. Traditional, alt.)

1. O come, little children, O come, one and all,
   To Bethlehem haste, to the manger so small;
   God's son for a gift has been sent us this night
   To be our Redeemer, our joy and delight.

2. He's born in a stable for you and for me,
   Draw near by the bright gleaming starlight to
       see
   How shepherds are kneeling with hearts full of
       love,
   While angels sing loud alleluias above.

3. Dear Christ Child, what gifts can we children
       bestow
   By which our affection and gladness we show?
   Our hearts, Lord, to you we will offter today,
   We offer them gladly; accept them, we pray.

O Little Town of Bethlehem

1. O little town of Bethlehem, how still we see
       thee lie;
   Above they deep and dreamless sleep the silent
       stars go by;
   Yet in thy dark streets shineth the Everlasting
       Light:
   The hopes and fears of all the years are met in
       thee tonight.

2. For Christ is born of Mary, and gathered all
      above,
   While mortals sleep, the angels keep their
      watch of wondering love.
   O morning stars, together proclaim the holy
      birth!
   And praises sing to God the King, and peace to
      men on earth!

3. How silently, how silently the wondrous gift is
      given!
   So God imparts to human hearts the blessings
      of his heaven;
   No ear may hear his coming, but in this world
      of sin,
   Where meek souls will receive him, still the
      dear Christ enters in.

4. O Holy Child of Bethlehem! descend to us, we
      pray;
   Cast out our sin and enter in, be born in us
      today.
   We hear the Christmas angels the great glad
      tidings tell;
   O come to us, abide with us, our Lord
      Emmanuel!

Phillips Brooks

Silent Night

1. Silent night, holy night,
   All is calm, all is bright
   Round yon virgin mother and child;
   Holy infant so tender and mild,
   Sleep in heavenly peace,
   Sleep in heavenly peace,

2. Silent night, holy night,
   Shepherds quake at the sight,
   Glories stream from heaven afar,
   Heavenly hosts sing alleluia;
   Christ, the Savior, is born!
   Christ, the Savior, is born!

3. Silent night, holy night,
   Son of God, love's pure light,
   Radiant beams from your holy face,
   With the dawn of redeeming grace,
   Jesus, Lord, at your birth,
   Jesus, Lord, at your birth.

Joseph Mohr

We Three Kings

1. We three kings of Orient are,
   Bearing gifts we traverse afar,
   Field and fountain, moor and mountain,
   Following yonder star.

   Refrain
   Oh, star of wonder, star of night,
   Star with royal beauty bright,

Westward leading, still proceeding,
Guide us to the perfect Light.

2. Born a babe on Bethlehem's plain,
Gold we bring to crown him again;
King for ever, ceasing never,
Over us all to reign.

Refrain

3. Frankincense to offer have I;
Incense owns a deity nigh,
Prayer and praising, all men raising,
Worship him, God on high.

Refrain

4. Myrrh is mine; its bitter perfume
Breathes a life of gathering gloom;
Sorrow, sighing, bleeding, dying,
Sealed in the stone-cold tomb.

Refrain

5. Glorious now behold him rise,
King and God and Sacrifice;
Heaven sings "Alleluia";
"Alleluia," earth replies.

Refrain

John H. Hopkins

What Child Is This?

1. What child is this, who, laid to rest,
   On Mary's lap is sleeping?
   Whom angels greet with anthems sweet,
   While shepherds watch are keeping?

   Refrain
   This, this is Christ the King,
   Whom shepherds guard and angels sing:
   Haste, haste to bring him laud,
   The babe, the son of Mary.

2. Why lies he in such mean estate
   Where ox and ass are feeding?
   Good Christian, fear; for sinners here
   The silent Word is pleading.

   Refrain
3. So bring him incense, gold, and myrrh,
   Come peasant, king, to own him,
   The King of kings salvation brings,
   Let loving hearts enthrone him.

   Refrain

William C. Dix